Planning and Budgeting for the Agile Enterprise

Planning and Budgeting for the Agile Enterprise

A Driver-Based Budgeting Toolkit

Richard Barrett

AMSTERDAM • BOSTON • HEIDELBERG • LONDON
NEW YORK • OXFORD • PARIS • SAN DIEGO
SAN FRANCISCO • SINGAPORE • SYDNEY • TOKYO
CIMA Publishing is an imprint of Elsevier

ELSEVIER

CIMA PUBLISHING

CIMA Publishing is an imprint of Elsevier
Linacre House, Jordan Hill, Oxford OX2 8DP
30 Corporate Drive, Suite 400, Burlington, MA 01803, USA

First edition 2007

Notice
No responsibility is assumed by the publisher for any injury and/or damage to persons
or property as a matter of products liability, negligence or otherwise, or from any use
or operation of any methods, products, instructions or ideas contained in the material
herein. Because of rapid advances in the medical sciences, in particular, independent
verification of diagnoses and drug dosages should be made

British Library Cataloguing in Publication Data
A catalogue record for this book is available from the British Library

Library of Congress Cataloguing in Publication Data
A catalog record for this title is available from the Library of Congress

ISBN–13: 978-0-7506-8327-2

For information on all CIMA Publishing publications
visit our website at http://www.cimapublishing.elsevier.com

Printed and bound in The Netherlands

07 08 09 10 11   10 9 8 7 6 5 4 3 2 1

Contents

Preface

Open any text book on management accounting and typically you will find a number of highly detailed chapters on cost management techniques, but very little on budgeting. This is quite interesting, especially when the budgeting process remains the pre-eminent mechanism for performance management in most organizations and is the most important interface between the finance function and the rest of the business. This lack of content may simply be a reflection of the fact that the budgeting process has not evolved much in the last seventy years. Inside most organizations it remains much as it was when it first came into prominence in the early part of the twentieth century.

During this time there has been some pioneering work on new approaches to budgeting. The Beyond Budgeting Round Table has identified the folly of rewarding employees for achieving negotiated fixed budgets and suggests basing bonuses and incentives on relative performance measures benchmarked against peer-group competitors or previous results. As such the people who should be paying attention to this message are the board and the human resources department rather than the finance function. The other notable advance is activity-based budgeting which grew out of activity-based costing and is now represented by a number of pioneering publications. However for most budget controllers, this approach remains complex and impenetrable, which possibly accounts for its low level of adoption.

Drowning under the plethora of spreadsheets that most organizations still use for budgeting, accountants will reach for almost any lifeline that is offered and this typically means a packaged budgeting application. Implementing these provides a ready solution to many of the pain points that the finance functions suffers in the annual round of budgeting and re-forecasting. Yet research suggests they do little to enable more frequent re-forecasting or to reduce the amount of time line managers inside the organizations spend on planning and budgeting. So what is to be done?

The purpose of this book is to offer a way forward. It contains little if any groundbreaking theory. It does not propose any radical changes in budgeting practices. Driver-based budgeting still requires the participation of line managers and still results in the usual chart of accounts and cash flow statements. Rather than being "big-bang", it is an approach that can be implemented incrementally so that organizations can grow into it as both line managers and the finance department gain confidence. As such, there is little, if any, risk involved. Many line managers already use some form of driver-based planning to generate some of the line item expenses that make up their budget submissions. Once they understand what is meant by driver-based budgeting, most will recognize it as something they already do and readily embrace the approach.

The challenge, therefore, clearly lies with the finance director, the budget controller and their colleagues in the finance department to work alongside business managers and bridge the gap between operational planning and enterprise budgeting. Uniting it into a single process brings untold benefits.

Acknowledgements

Few business practices are invented. Neither do they come into the world as a fully formed theory complete with a tried and trusted methodology. They seem to start with an individual or group of individuals working inside an organization. Frustrated with accepted practices, they go right back to the basics asking themselves questions about "what exactly are we trying to do here" and develop new ways of tackling old problems. Their solution works for them in their situation and spreads by word of mouth inside their organization as well as outside into other organizations as people move jobs. Eventually an academic or lowly writer like me documents and labels the idea and from that point on it takes a life of its own. This is certainly the way that activity-based costing came into the world and one suspects that the conception of a host of other accounting practices such as economic value added and the balanced scorecard, that are now closely associated with a single organization or an individual, started life in a similar manner. This is not to decry the work of academics. They bring much needed rigour to adolescent concepts; researching best practice and eventually fleshing out a more complete methodology. But rarely are the academics the real heroes.

That honour lies with the unsung mavericks who first thought of doing something different. They are the people who really deserve our respect. They may not even be aware that they were doing anything innovative; it just made sense and worked for them. They may not even be unique with hundreds of independent minds across the globe simultaneously stumbling on a similar approach. I suspect that is what happened with the methodology that has now come to be labelled driver-based budgeting. Twenty years ago when I was working as planning manager at the express delivery company, DHL Worldwide Express, the annual budget was produced using a driver-based approach and I would like to acknowledge my colleagues from those days – Patrick Byron, Brian Taylor, James Darnton and Tony Hodgson. I doubt whether they would ever assume to have invented driver-based budgeting though. Neither would André Lam who had developed a driver-based approach to revenue planning at Petplan, the world's largest small animal insurer where I spent the next stage of my career.

After two decades of holding down commercial roles that involved the significant use of sophisticated cost and profitability reporting and some different perspectives on planning and budgeting, I found a role into the software industry. This allows me to work alongside some evangelists who are intent on improving planning and budgeting today. These people come from within the software industry; from inside organizations that are seeking to transform their planning, budgeting and re-forecasting practices, and from business schools and industry consortia. Knowingly or unknowingly, many of them have contributed to the development of this book. I would particularly like to thank my colleagues – Steve Mainprize, Jim Robinson and Mike Sherratt – who helped me to distil my ideas and diligently reviewed the draft; Cathy Jorgensen of Fortis Health, Paul Witham of TNT Express UK, David Hart of BDL Hotels and David Weller of WHSmith Retail for spending the time to share their experiences; Dr Mike Bourne of Cranfield University School of Management for investing his time drafting some of the case studies and finally Ashok Vadgama, his colleagues and participants at CAM-I, the Consortium of Advanced Management, International, both for allowing me to reproduce the diagram of the CAM-I Closed Loop in Chapter 5 and for providing such a valuable arena for organizations to meet and work together to develop best practice across a wide range of performance management issues. My thanks also go to David Blansfield, Editor of *Business Finance* Magazine and the Publisher, Penton, for allowing me to reproduce their write-up of Western Container Services in Chapter 3.

My thanks also go to Janice Howard and Evanna Morris at the Chartered Institute of Management Accountants for helping establish the CIMA Mastercourse on implementing driver-based budgeting; to Mike Cash at Elsevier for the readiness with which he picked up on my unsolicited suggestion for this book and to Jonathan Gunning and Sumitha Nithyanandan for their professional support during the production process.

Finally, my deepest thanks to my wife Cindy and our children, Eleanor and Jolyon, who provided the support and encouragement to complete this book.

Introduction

The traditional view of business has the senior management team as the captains of the ship. They stand at the helm, gaze out towards the horizon and occasionally refer back to highly reliable marine charts and tide tables. The wind and currents may blow the ship off course, but by keeping a regular watch, they can continue to steam towards their chosen destination with no more than a few degrees of correction to port or starboard. If there are no obvious perils in sight, they can go below, relax and pass the port. The day-to-day life of most executives is not like this; nor has it been for the last few decades. Their daily existence most resembles that of white-water kayaker racing down a fast unfamiliar river in a fog. They spend all of their time staying afloat and avoiding the dangers that keep leaping out of the gloom, but they cannot leave the current and rest in an eddy because the competition is right behind them. In a moment's distraction they will capsize and someone will overtake them.

In today's uncertain and fast changing world, sound strategy, good people and world-class processes only count for so much and success or failure are likely to be determined by factors that are outside of our control. There is a myriad of external factors such as technology, competition, regulation, consumer preferences and economics that combine in complex ways to throw up opportunities and threats. We cannot predict what form they will take or how long they will last. The same goes for relative strengths and weaknesses. What we once considered a sustainable competitive advantage can evaporate overnight as an off-the-radar competitor changes the rules of the game. In this environment, long-range planning is positively dangerous, especially when it leads companies to make large investments in fixed and inflexible assets. We can map out the most likely scenarios and develop a handful of strategies and contingency plans. But ultimately we have to learn to live with uncertainty.

Uncertainty is not the same as risk. Risk resides in simple choices to which probabilities can be assigned by statistically analysing past observations. Investors can collect and analyse data on the performance of stock across a large number of companies, markets and time periods, and estimate probabilities for the likely return on their investment. Gamblers know that there are only thirty-eight possible places a roulette ball can come to rest. Uncertainty is much messier. Executives cannot foresee every possible outcome of their actions. The timing, sequence and combination of external and internal events present too many possible outcomes to evaluate and before any thorough assessment could be made as to the best course of action, a new set of circumstances would present themselves. These could include new competitors appearing from out of left field; regulations changing; consumer preferences shifting; commodity prices and interest rates fluctuating wildly, to say nothing of geopolitical events, natural disasters and existing competitors doing their utmost to thwart the best laid plans. Compared with their investors who simply have to decide whether to buy or sell stock, managers have it tough. They have to cope with uncertainty.

Sometimes, as Donald Sull[1] points out in his writings on mastering uncertainty, managers attempt to deal with uncertainty by turning a messy situation into a big bet. Marconi did this when it attempted to transform itself with a string of disposals and acquisitions. The European telecommunication providers did this when they paid €100 billion for third-generation (3G) mobile technology licenses. For these bets on 3G to be successful, a myriad of things would have needed to happen differently. Regulators would have needed to change policy on competition and returns on capital, the development of competing technologies would have needed to be different from what it is today and the competitive landscape would need to evolve in another way. With the benefit of hindsight, it is easy to gloat and pick holes in the decisions that managers in both Marconi and the telecommunications sector made. But reality is such that managers have to manage forwards and make decisions about an uncertain future.

Uncertain markets present a seemingly endless stream of opportunities and threats some of which will turn out to be insubstantial and unsustainable while others evolve in ways that transform the competitive landscape. Established players have little choice other than to quickly adapt to the changing market conditions before they become an anomaly. Think of Kodak which is surviving by investing heavily to reinvent itself for the digital age, while classic camera company Leica looks increasingly vulnerable. As Charles Darwin noted, it is not the strongest of the species that survive, nor is it the most intelligent. It is those that are most adaptable to change.

In order to be adaptable, organizations need to equip themselves with two distinct capabilities: better visibility into the murky uncertain future and greater agility to execute effectively and efficiently. These capabilities have to be systematically developed, just like the skills of our white-water kayaker. From past experience they can quickly read the water and execute the right paddle stroke to move the kayak so they take advantage of the quickest and safest passage. Inevitably the force of the water will occasionally cause them to lose their balance, but with a repertoire of almost autonomic support strokes to call upon, they seldom capsize. Even when they do, their ability to execute an Eskimo roll is programmed into their muscles and they are up and on their way in no time. But critically they are never totally focused on their immediate surroundings always giving themselves time to look down the river and work out where to position themselves and what strokes to use for the next series of obstacles. It is the same capabilities that organizations need today; visibility of what lies ahead and the agility to deal with it quickly and efficiently.

Among the many things that organizations need to put in place to be better able to deal with unpredictability are systems and processes that provide better visibility into the future, and responsiveness and agility in execution. At the strategic level, visibility comes from systematically scanning the external market and everything that might possibly impact it, looking for patterns and inconsistencies that might suggest the germs of an opportunity or threat. The data is necessarily incomplete, fleeting and frequently contradictory. In the short term, all the assumptions that an organization has about its markets and its ability to achieve its financial goals are set out in its annual budget. This short-term view needs to be constantly revisited both to identify any early warning signals that might indicate that the assumptions that underpin longer-term strategy no longer hold true and to fine tune current year performance. Research reported in Chapter 3 clearly shows that companies do not re-forecast as frequently as they would like which compromises their visibility into the future.

The failure to re-forecast regularly also compromises organizational agility. In this context, agility is the ability to sense changes in both the external environment and the internal organization, and respond appropriately and efficiently to those changes. Sometimes this might mean simply realigning resources and expenses to a new level of trading; at other times it might mean doing things differently or perhaps even fine-tuning strategy. New business initiatives need close monitoring to ensure they are on track to deliver tomorrow's cash flows and to detect any tipping point when they need to be rapidly scaled to take advantage of a window of opportunity. Today's core businesses need a similar level of attention to make sure they deliver today's profits and the cash that will fund innovation in the future. Frequent re-forecasting and dynamic budgets are therefore one of the key building blocks of the agile organization. But currently most organizations are caught in a logjam. They want to re-forecast more frequently, but their current planning and budgeting process are so laborious that even those that have purchased packaged budgeting applications are still no better off than those that budget on spreadsheets.

This is because there is little integration between operational planning and enterprise budgeting. The former is done by line managers with their spreadsheet models hidden away on their desktops while the latter is done by the finance department on their enterprise budgeting systems. The concept of driver-based budgeting as a way of spanning this void is developed in Chapter 5 and a discussion of its relative strengths and weaknesses follows in Chapter 6. Shared services functions are a substantial part of the cost base in many organizations and Chapter 7 examines ways in which planning and budgeting in these support functions can be encompassed in a driver-based budget.

The final chapters focus on how to go about implementing driver-based budgeting, first examining ways of cost justifying the investment, then looking at the type of systems that are required to support a driver-based budgeting solution before working through the specific issues that are faced when implementing this type of budgeting. The appendices includes interviews with members of pioneering organizations that have implemented a driver-based approach to planning and budgeting.

Notes

1   "Mastering Uncertainty", *Financial Times Supplement*, 12 March 2006.

2

The Re-forecasting Dilemma

Many organizations want to streamline their budgeting process; some want to eliminate it completely. Regardless of what their endgame might be, producing more frequent re-forecasts is typically part of the solution. Research[1] suggests that many companies recognize the need to re-forecast more frequently, including many of those who currently re-forecast every quarter. But before getting involved in a headlong pursuit for more frequent re-forecasting, organizations should take a step back and work out what makes sense for them, given the volatility of their market, the external factors that impact them and their ability to increase or decrease resources at short notice.

When to re-forecast?

Re-forecasting year-end results

Most companies re-forecast their current year-end results at some point during their financial year; many do this as they start the annual planning and budgeting cycle. Some companies will re-forecast quarterly doing a 3+9, 6+6 and 9+3 review – the first number denoting the number of months to date and the second number denoting the number of months to go until the fiscal year end. In shorthand this is YTD and YTG. Regardless of the frequency of these re-forecasts, they are singularly focused on establishing if the year-end targets will be met, or if not, what short-term actions can be taken to reduce expenditure and get the organization back on track. While re-forecasting year-end results undoubtedly helps companies towards delivering the profitability they have promised to their investors and managers towards the bonuses that come as part of their benefits packages, short-term expense management can disrupt finely honed strategies designed to create longer-term value. Occasionally an overzealous focus on delivering short-term results drives management teams towards actions they later regret as was the case with SSL International plc, the UK-based medical goods manufacturer, that purposefully overstocked their distributors in order to fill a short fall in year-end revenues. In the following year when they had to wait for the estimated £63 million worth of stock to wash through the supply chain resulting in a one-off loss of profit of approximately £50 million, confidence in the company collapsed and the share price followed.[2]

This is an extreme case. Most of the actions taken to achieve year-end targets are simply disruptive and any negative impact they may have on creating long-term shareholder value cannot be detected externally. Businesses do not wind down towards Christmas, stop abruptly on 31st December and start a new on 1st January from a clean sheet of paper. The sales orders that were taken in December will need fulfilling; the customer retention issue that was first noticed in quarter 3 will continue to have its detrimental effect on future revenues, and the temporary staff recruited in customer accounts in October will still be needed in the new year to bring down the days outstanding. We may use 31st December or 31st March as the cut-off for reporting externally to shareholders and regulators, but internally these dates have no more importance than any other month end.

Rolling re-forecasts

Re-forecasting on a rolling basis helps overcome such short-term thinking. A rolling re-forecast looks out into the future for a fixed number of periods, regardless of the current period. So if an organization has adopted a 12-monthly rolling re-forecasts, in May managers will re-forecast revenues and expenses for the periods June to the following May. Then in June they will re-forecast for the periods July to the following June. Each time management gets sight of the bigger picture for the next 12 months as another month is added to the schedule. But with each re-forecast, managers are firming up their forecasts for the remaining months of the current fiscal year, providing the board with the forward visibility in year-end results that they need to provide guidance to analysts tracking their stock.

At the beginning of May, managers will be provided with reports covering revenues and expenses for each period for the current year to date together with their most recent forecasts for each period through to the following April. They already provided figures for each of these months in the preceding month, so they just need reviewing and updating. However, this should not be skimped. Managers should be encouraged to spend half their time focusing on the next 6 months to ensure these numbers are as accurate as possible. One way to motivate them to do this is to provide them with regular feedback on the accuracy of their past forecasts. For instance, they can be provided with analysis of the accuracy of their forecasting for the most recent month, which in this case is April. By doing this managers will be able to monitor whether the accuracy of their forecasts improves each month, until with only a month to go, the last forecast provided in March should have been pretty nearly spot on. Providing such feedback encourages managers to strive for greater accuracy and helps the finance function to focus its resources on cost centres and departments whose forecasts are persistently adrift of the eventual outcomes. Any company that reports financial results on a quarterly basis can find that even a small shortfall in earnings per share has a disproportionate effect on stock price. In such a situation anything that can be done to improve the accuracy of forecasts will be worthwhile.

How far should you look ahead

Using rolling re-forecasts fails to make much sense if anything less than a 12-month time horizon is used. In fact many companies that have adopted rolling re-forecasts look forward 18 months; the rationale being that once they have got to the sixth month of their current fiscal year, they have full visibility of their next fiscal year. Some have adopted even longer time horizons, blurring any distinction between operational budgeting and strategic planning and examples of this are discussed in later chapters.

How frequently should you re-forecast

There are a few rule-of-thumb assumptions about how often organizations need to re-forecast. These are based on the level of predictability in the markets they compete in, the amount of resource the company has to weather short-term fluctuations in earnings and the time horizon of the their businesses. These will be examined in turn to see whether they have any foundation.

Companies that compete in markets that are characterized by higher levels of uncertainty ought to re-forecast more frequently than companies that compete in markets that are more stable

Budgets are based on a myriad of assumptions. Some of these will be explicit and shared by the board, the executive and operational managers. For instance:

- An insurer may have produced their budget on the assumption that their competitors will all want to improve their profitability and not discount so deeply in the coming year. This will lead to an improvement in customer retention and an increase in average premiums.
- A mobile network provider may have forecast their revenue growth based on assumptions about the predicted growth in text messaging. However, industry experts cannot agree how rapid this growth will be.

- An express delivery company may have forecast their expenses based on assumptions about fuel costs which have been fluctuating recently due to renewed political unrest in major oil producing economies.

Other assumptions might be less explicit and less visible. Some may only be known to a single responsibility centre manager. Somewhere in the company a key account sales manager may have forecast his sales revenue on the assumption that he will be able to win a new customer to replace the one who gave him notice last quarter. These assumptions need monitoring during the course of the financial year and that means re-forecasting both revenue and expenses on a regular basis.

Companies that have enough resources to ride out periodic fluctuations in their income do not need to re-forecast as frequently as companies with limited resources

No one would dispute that a company with a large cash pile sufficient to pay salaries and suppliers when revenues are low or non-existent can continue to trade for longer than a company with little cash. Similarly no one would dispute that during periods of uncertainty a company with access to additional sources of capital could continue to trade for longer than a company whose investors and lenders have pulled the plug on any further investment.

However, although such companies can survive for longer without regular forecasts, it is not in anyone's interests not to review and re-forecast their financial performance. The executive still needs to identify the underlying cause for any poor performance, project future revenues and expenses and assess exactly how long their current cash will last and when they might need to seek additional funding. The sooner they do this the better. Not only will they be able to identify and implement some quick actions to optimize short-term profitability, but they will be able to keep their investors and lenders informed of the situation and together identify how much additional funding may be required and when it may be called upon. Investors, market analysts and lenders all dislike sudden surprises and any company that fails to provide regular guidance on its future earnings or funding requirements does nothing to inspire their confidence. Their response can take many forms all of which are detrimental to stakeholders. Investors can show their disdain by selling their stock, and analysts can mark down the stock. Lenders prepared to provide additional funding will probably want a higher interest rate to reflect the perceived risk, effectively increasing the company's cost of capital. Re-forecasting regularly and keeping everyone fully informed of the situation at the earliest opportunity would preclude many of these events from happening.

But the failure to re-forecast regularly may mean that more fundamental issues go undetected and unaddressed for longer. Any company that is resource-rich has evidently been successful in the past. Senior managers will have built up a shared understanding of how their market operates and what they have to do to satisfy the needs of consumers. This shared understanding will have served them well, helping them hit their targets and earn their bonuses every year. It will have given them the confidence to ignore upstart competitors who "don't understand this market" or "won't last long selling at those prices". On many occasions in the past events will have unfolded exactly as they anticipated and this will have reinforced their belief in the validity of their understanding of their market and the way it works.

However things change. Markets that were once predictable start to behave differently. The upstart competitor who theoretically should have collapsed long ago just keeps growing and is rumoured to be trading profitably. Could they really be sourcing product of that quality so cheaply? Or is it because they are covering the whole of Europe from a single warehouse? Either way, something has changed that looks to have invalidated everyone's shared understanding of the way this market has operated for the past decade or more.

Managers cannot ignore seemingly short-term hiccups in their financial performance. They need to treat it as a possible early warning sign of a more fundamental change in their market and investigate it accordingly. This means identifying exactly what caused it and how longer-term profitability will be impacted if the situation endures. If revenue fell short of projections simply due to delays in production and a backlog of unfulfilled orders, then as long as the situation can be recovered before customers defect due to poor service, it is likely to be a short-term problem. Finance will need to work with the production planners to see when normal supply will be resumed and re-forecast revenue and expenses accordingly, perhaps recognizing that there is likely to be a significant increase in labour costs for the next few months. But if revenue fell because customers of all sizes are defecting to the new upstart competitor, it is likely to be a major problem that will take some time to sort out. It could mean moving production to a location where labour would be cheaper. It could mean rationalizing the supply chain. Either way, time is likely to be precious.

Even in markets that were previously stable, managers should recognize that short-term blips in profitability could be early warning signs that tectonic plates are beginning to rub against one another and there could soon be a seismic change in their market. Regardless of how cash-rich a company may be, any distant rumblings and short-term incongruities should be treated as a sign that something more fundamental could be happening. Managers need to identify the underlying causality, revise the assumptions that underpin their planning and re-forecast their revenues and expenses. The old adage of "Fail to plan; Plan to fail" excludes no one.

Companies that compete in markets with long lead times and extended time horizons do not need to re-forecast as frequently as those that compete in markets with shorter time horizons

The media love to side with outraged taxpayers when it is suddenly announced that a capital project that is scheduled to take a number of years to complete is over budget. In recent history, the Millennium Dome, the Scottish Parliament Building and the new Wembley Stadium have all gone spectacularly above their original estimates and each time there has been a public outcry. It is unlikely that the public is appalled at the overspend, as they surely appreciated that there must be some element of finger in the wind when it comes to estimating construction costs from an architect's plans and specifications. It is more likely they are taken aback by the seeming suddenness of such announcements. Just like investors and market analysts, the public do not like surprises involving large amounts of money. Rightly or wrongly, they smell incompetence as they know from their own experience in managing their family finances, that if you keep a regular track on your personal expenditure, bank and credit card statements hold few surprises. If they can do this, why can't the project managers running these large construction projects.

One hopes that such projects are diligently managed with project managers constantly asking suppliers, contractors and sub-contractors for regular re-forecasts of likely timescales and costs so they know very early on that overspends are likely. Could it be that it is the politicians who are keeping this information out of the public domain in the forlorn hope that somehow the project will be brought back on track without any embarrassment? No matter, we have squashed another myth about re-forecasting. No matter what timescales underpin decision making in a business, there are benefits from more frequent forecasting.

In North America there is anecdotal evidence of some companies that only close their accounts every 3 months in order to produce their quarterly earnings reports. This leaves them 2 months with ample time for thinking about the future, re-forecasting and reviewing business issues. As 2 months is the longest period between a re-forecast and having actual results, there are few surprises and cutting non-value-adding historic reporting to free up time to focus on the future makes sound business sense.

The cost–benefit model of re-forecasting frequency

If none of these commonly accepted rules of thumb about how frequently a company should re-forecast appears to stand up to detailed scrutiny, where does that leave us? Should a company just re-forecast when things are not going to plan? If revenue is falling below projections and expenses are running away with themselves, there is certainly a pressing need for managers to identify some spending cuts and forecast what the coming months will look like. Sometimes when cash reserves are running low, it is simply a matter of keeping the creditors at bay and fighting for survival. Or should a company re-forecast every now and again just to ensure everything is on track for achieving the annual bonus? Many do and if their remuneration packages include a bonus for achieving a pre-negotiated revenue or profit target, managers would be foolish not to. Or lured by what is often presented as best practice, perhaps all companies should work towards adopting rolling monthly re-forecasts?

Who knows? When it comes to re-forecasting there are no right or wrong answers. The only sure thing one can say is that if you are going to re-forecast, make sure it is worth the effort. Let us start from the basic principle that the value gained from doing a re-forecast should be greater than the cost of doing the re-forecast. For instance, doing a re-forecast may identify the opportunity to realign resources with new levels of trading and reduce operating expenses. If these savings exceed the cost of doing the re-forecast then the exercise created value and was worth doing. Alternatively, doing a re-forecast might reveal an opportunity for additional sales and if the incremental profit of these sales exceeds the cost of doing the re-forecast, again the re-forecast was worth doing.

Adopting such a value-based approach to the frequency of re-forecasting helps focus on the key issues:

- The amount of time that members of the finance function and line managers invest in producing a re-forecast has a cost associated with it. If they were not doing the re-forecast, they could be doing something more useful. For instance, one of the key elements of any re-forecast is the revenue and taking salespeople away from face-to-face selling time has to be worth it. So in some instances, the saving is an opportunity cost. But in other instances such as where headcount is saved in the finance function, it is a bankable cost-saving.

- If a company only does a single re-forecast during their financial year, they are likely to gain more value from it than a company that has adopted monthly rolling re-forecasting does from any one of its monthly forecasting cycles. The opportunities to identify expense savings are much greater. Put simply, the more frequently an organisation re-forecasts, the less value it is likely to realize from each round of re-forecasting. It is the law of diminishing returns.

If re-forecasting is a laborious and time-consuming exercise involving a large community of contributors as well as a considerable amount of effort in the finance department, the opportunity cost is likely to be considerable. If a re-forecast involves a hundred managers who spend an entire day to review and re-forecast their expenses, the exercise consumes 100 man-days. As there are only 220 working days in a typical calendar year, it adds up to half the annual salary and benefits package of one of these managers. If the cost of the finance department in coordinating and consolidating the re-forecast is included, the total cost involved becomes sizeable. It is hardly a compelling argument to justify more frequent re-forecasts!

However, if these 100 managers only spent an hour each month re-forecasting, this opportunity cost is reduced by a factor of 7 or 8. Then moving to monthly rolling re-forecasts might be viable as the value gained from each round of re-forecasting is more likely to outweigh the opportunity cost. This challenge to continually derive value from more frequent re-forecasting is represented in the diagram shown in Figure 2.1 below.

Given the current cost of each re-forecast, the optimal frequency is represented in the diagram by the point, F^1. However, if the cost can be substantially reduced with managers spending an hour rather than a day doing their re-forecasts each month, then the optimal frequency is increased and is represented in the diagram by the new point, F^2.

Given this relationship, the debate about re-forecasting is no longer a discussion about what is appropriate for companies in a particular market sector or for companies involved in business with particular time horizons. The determining

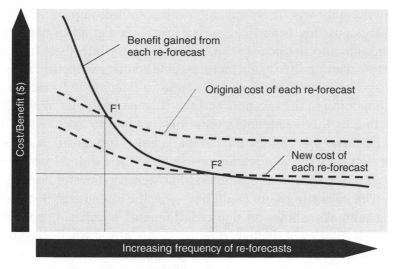

Figure 2.1   The optimal frequency of re-forecasts based on value

factor is the opportunity cost of re-forecasting and the challenge for the future is to reduce this cost. Put simply, if re-forecasting can be made quicker and cheaper, there is value from doing it more frequently.

Who should re-forecast?

Many companies know that the cost of involving the whole management team in regular re-forecasting is prohibitive. That is why many leave it to the finance department. There is no doubt that an experienced financial analyst can look at the management accounts for previous periods and make a quick assessment about the remaining periods until the end of the financial year. If one group of products has been consistently performing above budget, they will mark that up for the coming months. If a particular line item expense has been running below budget, they will mark that down. Each time they will be using what is colloquially referred to as the "burn rate". This term comes from rocket engineering and refers to the amount of fuel consumed to cover a measured distance. So if the company got to June and expenses have been consistently running 3% below budget each period, why not use this "burn rate" and mark down expenses for the remaining periods by 3% as well? Many organizations say they already practice monthly rolling re-forecasting. But when questioned further, it often turns out that it is not an enterprise-wide process, just someone in the finance department projecting historic "burn rates" across future periods.

Is there anything inherently wrong or dangerous in this approach? On the positive side, it is possibly better than not re-forecasting at all in that it provides senior managers and the board with better visibility into their future performance so they can provide their investors and lenders with regular guidance. However, this will only happen if the new re-forecast is based on what is actually happening in the business and the finance team may not have a good understanding of this. Undoubtedly the best people to ask what is happening in the business are the operational managers. That means people such as the senior managers in the marketing department, the individual key account managers who talk with their customers almost every day and the head of procurement. The marketing team might have specific knowledge that their costly advertising campaign shows no sign of influencing purchasing behaviour and this will result in sales of the new product range falling woefully short of projections. An individual key account manager might know that she is just about to secure a major contract with one of her clients and it will mean production going into overdrive for the remainder of the year. The procurement manager might know that when he comes to re-negotiate his most important contract, he is not going to match the price he was expecting when he prepared his budget 8 months ago.

The finance department could easily be oblivious to all this local knowledge. At best, everything could work out well and the eventual financial results could be better than the finance department's re-forecast. Perhaps some things will work out well and some things work out badly leaving the results not far removed from the finance department's re-forecast. But there is a chance that everything could work out badly and the company ends up adrift of the re-forecast. This is the risk associated with relying on the finance department to re-forecast. In fact what is being done is not forecasting so much as simple trending. Unless managers who are directly involved in running the business are consulted, many of the critical internal or external factors that influence future revenues and expenses may be ignored. So although most of the time there may be no discernable issues with having only the finance department produce re-forecasts when it goes wrong it has the potential to go dramatically wrong. The only sure way to produce reliable re-forecasts is to involve the line managers. But do they all need to be involved all of the time?

Who to involve in rolling re-forecasts

Because the expenses controlled by cost centre managers in departments such as facilities tend to be highly predictable across the year, it is often suggested that they can be excluded from rolling re-forecasts and only those managers responsible for revenue and large elements of controllable costs need be routinely involved. This common-sense approach means doing a Pareto analysis, adopting the 80/20 rule, and focusing on the handful of departments and handful of line items that have the biggest impact on revenues and expenses. The suggestion is that only these departmental managers need get involved in re-forecasting.

But on further examination, there is no valid reason to exclude these functions from more frequent re-forecasting. On many occasions the managers in charge of these departments will simply review their line item expenses and resubmit them unchanged. This activity should take them a few minutes at most and if this is all it takes, it is hardly a valid reason to exclude them. But there are actually important reasons why they should be routinely included in every round of re-forecasting. Managers of support functions – such as facilities, HR and IT – make decisions that involve step changes in capacity and have implications for many years into the future. To be able to make informed decisions, these managers need good forward visibility of non-financial operational data, such as headcount and the anticipated number of new recruits. That way they can optimize the resources under their control in the short term, perhaps reorganizing existing space to accommodate an increase in headcount, as well as having adequate lead time to plan for any new facility that may be needed in the longer term.

The advent of web-based enterprise planning and budgeting applications and work management tools means that all managers can be involved in the re-forecasting process with little or no extra effort or cost. If after perusing their previous re-forecast they see no need for change, they can simply resubmit it. They may not have made any amendments, but they will have had the opportunity to review any assumptions that underpin their future plans. At some point in the future, they will actually need to put their plans into action. So if the budgeting and re-forecasting process is efficient and there is little additional cost, there are definite benefits from involving everybody all the time.

What to re-forecast?

When asking departmental managers for a re-forecast, finance departments typically send out a schedule that includes the complete set of line items. Managers comply with this request and somewhat blindly re-forecast every line item on the schedule regardless of whether it is a large enough expense to have any impact on their departmental total, yet alone the organization's total expense budget. Going to this level of detail is clearly a waste of time.

When re-forecasting, departmental managers need to focus on those things that are likely to change and have a significant impact on revenue or expenditure in future periods. There is little need to rework travelling expenses or stationery; just leave them alone. Instead managers should be asked to concentrate on the handful of line items that are significant, volatile and where they have some level of control. Undoubtedly this will mean spending time in re-forecasting line items such as the revenue, controllable staff costs and marketing expenses. Many other line items are too insignificant to warrant consideration.

Some managers are smart enough to do just this. When they are asked to re-forecast their expenses they go straight to the line items they know really matter and leave the rest unchanged. But having analysed the impact of particular line items in the past, the finance department and senior operations managers could agree which line items are most important and label them with a code in the budgeting system to tell managers exactly where to direct their attention. Those line items labelled "A" should be rigorously re-forecast on every occasion; those labelled "B" should be re-forecast if actual expenditure for the year to date has exceeded the budgeted expenditure by x%, and those labelled "C" should only ever be re-forecast if actual expenditure for the year to date has exceeded the budgeted expenditure by y%. It is up to the finance department and the senior managers to suggest what "x" and "y" should be, but their aim should be to end up with no more than 10% of line items in category "A", 25% in category "B" and the remainder in category "C". Taking the time to develop such a categorization will make re-forecasting quicker so that it is less costly and give it a more commercial focus.

Summary

There are a number of commonly held rules of thumb about re-forecasting; none of which stand up to detailed scrutiny. There are no textbook recommendations about how frequently to re-forecast, how far to look forward or who to involve in the process. Faced with inefficient processes, many organizations make compromises, re-forecasting infrequently or getting finance to make top line adjustments based on "burn rates". There are some short-term gains that can be made from simple measures such as limiting re-forecasts to key line items. However, if more frequent re-forecasting is to create value for the organization, then the benefits that derive from doing a re-forecast should always be greater than the opportunity cost involved. Adopting this perspective suggests that re-forecasting should be treated like any other business process and subjected to the same process improvement and process management techniques to make it more efficient and less costly.

Notes

1   The Re-forecasting Survey 2002–2005 is an independent survey carried out annually by ALG Software and sponsored by the Chartered Institute of Management Accountants. It is available at www.algsoftware.com.
2   The history of the impact of the "trade loading" at SSL International plc can be followed by reading through the press releases the company issued starting on 24 May 2001. This can be found at www.ssl-international.com. Although criminal proceedings were bought against individuals in the company, the Serious Fraud Office failed to find sufficient evidence to bring a successful prosecution and the case was dropped. As the press releases show, a number of board members and senior executives were subsequently replaced as were the external auditors.

The Logjam with Re-forecasting

In the light of an upward trend in the number of companies issuing profit warnings and the steadily growing uncertainty that is a characteristic of an increasing number of markets; one would expect companies to be investing in new planning and budgeting applications so they can re-forecast their financial performance more frequently. Every year, Boston-based IT analyst IDC produces an estimate of the dollar value of the global market for planning and budgeting software produced by consolidating survey returns solicited from the individual software vendors. In 2004, IDC estimated this market to be worth US$599 million and to have grown by 15% during that year making it the largest and most dynamic sector of the global market for financial management software. Confident that companies will continue to be frustrated with their moribund planning and budgeting processes over the coming years, IDC predicts that this market will continue to enjoy double-figure growth for most of the decade. Other software sectors, such as Financial Reporting, might have enjoyed temporary blips as listed companies addressed the requirements of legislations such as the USA's Sarbanes–Oxley Act and the International Financial Reporting Standards. But buoyancy in this sector was short-lived and it has again acquiesced in a replacement market that is unlikely and unable to provide software vendors with the ever-expanding revenues and profits their investors demand. For them, there is only one market sector that really matters and that is planning and budgeting.

Software vendors have consistently spent millions of dollars on sales and marketing activity convincing Chief Financial Officers (CFOs) and their teams that their frustration and dissatisfaction with their planning and budgeting process could be a history if only they would implement new software and hand over the dollars for the licence fee. International Data Corporation's estimate of the value of this market suggests that everyone involved ought to be very happy. The software vendors have found a large and enduring stream of revenues and having handed over the dollars for the software, and possibly as much again for implementation services, organizations have had all their planning and budgeting issues resolved. What was once a slow and laborious process has been transformed giving companies the speed and dynamism they were seeking.

Although there are isolated reports of companies that have implemented new planning and budgeting software and subsequently slashed their budgeting cycle by weeks and occasionally months, the findings of quantitative research studies into the planning and budgeting performance of large companies have only revealed small incremental changes and certainly nothing that would warrant being labelled "transformational".

Debunking the myths about planning and budgeting

In 2005 the UK's Chartered Institute of Management Accountants has sponsored a research project into budgeting and re-forecasting practices amongst a sample of the UK's 1000 largest companies[1] – the respondents being the senior financial managers who were previously identified as being responsible for managing the budgeting process within their organizations. Nothing about the questions or methodology in the research study is unique and you can find numerous other studies asking similar questions. What is unique is that the survey has been run consistently for four consecutive years and is now capable of providing considerable insight into how planning and budgeting practices are changing at a time when many organizations are implementing new systems.

Myth 1: Because companies want better visibility into future financial performance they are re-forecasting more frequently

There is an almost universal recognition of the need to re-forecast. Ninety-one per cent of the respondents surveyed in 2005 reported that their organizations re-forecast their budgets at least once during their financial year and this figure has been steadily increasing over the last 3 years; this change being seen in the smaller (£500m, US$850m) organizations as well as in the larger ones.

The report also revealed that a quarter of these organizations were re-forecasting every month; some of these re-forecasting a rolling 12 or more months, some simply re-forecasting the remaining months until their financial year end. In addition, 51% of respondents reported that they would like to re-forecast more

Table 3.1 Current and desired frequency of re-forecasts, 2002–2005

		Quarterly	Monthly	Weekly	Daily
Current	2002	36%	24%	0%	0%
	2003	38%	24%	0%	0%
	2004	42%	25%	–	–
	2005	34%	26%	–	–
Desired	2002	33%	44%	5%	1%
	2003	36%	45%	3%	1%
	2004	37%	51%	1%	1%
	2005	38%	47%	3%	1%

frequently with many of these aiming to re-forecast monthly. However, despite this recognition of the need to re-forecast more frequently there has been little progress towards it during the 4 years that this survey has been run. Roughly half of the respondents stated that monthly re-forecasting is their desired frequency. However over the 4 years of the survey the proportion of companies achieving this has increased by only 2 percentage points, i.e. from 24 to 26%. The figures in Table 3.1 show the limited amount of progress being made.

Myth 2: Companies that have invested in packaged budgeting applications are likely to be re-forecasting more frequently than companies using spreadsheets as their enterprise planning and budgeting application

During the 4 years of the survey, there has been a marked change in the type of applications used for collecting and collating budget data. In 2002, 74% of respondents reported that spreadsheets were the main tool used for budgeting. By 2005, this figure had dropped to 49% reflecting significant financial investment in new software. Anyone who has been employed as a management accountant inside any large organization in recent years will be well aware of this. Although they may not have made the move away from spreadsheets themselves, they will have been the target of numerous marketing campaigns warning them of the perils and perversity of using spreadsheets for enterprise budgeting. At times the feeling of guilt and inadequacy must have been intolerable! No wonder many succumbed and implemented package applications.

The obvious question is whether this level of investment in new systems is enabling organizations to re-forecast more frequently. To provide the answer, current practices were compared between those organizations using spreadsheets and those using packaged budgeting systems. The results in Figure 3.1 clearly show that those organizations that have moved away from spreadsheets are not re-forecasting any more frequently than those organizations continuing to use them. Indeed a greater proportion of the organizations using spreadsheets were re-forecasting monthly. These findings suggest that simply investing on new software does little to enable an organization to re-forecast more frequently.

This is not to dismiss or denigrate the positive benefits that many organizations have gained from moving off spreadsheets to a packaged budgeting application

Planning and Budgeting using spreadsheets

Collecting and consolidating individual expense budgets into an enterprise budget involves a number of steps, each of them individually time-consuming and prone to errors:

1. First, someone in the finance department has got to set out the master budget spreadsheet. This may involve adding new line items and involve amending numerous formulas.
2. Once the master budget spreadsheet has been agreed, it has got to be copied for each business division or department sometimes adding another level of consolidation. In some companies this can mean hundreds of individual spreadsheets and numerous levels of consolidation.
3. Formulas have to be written in the master budget spreadsheet to consolidate the individual spreadsheets.
4. Some helpful finance departments will pre-populate these spreadsheets with current year actuals and previous year actuals so that the individual cost centre manager has some history to work with.
5. The individual spreadsheets will be e-mailed to the departmental managers. As this is a manual process, it is quite easy to miss a department completely or to mistakenly send a pre-populated spreadsheet to the wrong cost centre manager. At best, all that has been wasted is time and effort. At worst, the manager opens the spreadsheets and discovers that his supposed co-worker has a better benefits package and he storms off to complain to his superior. Finance will probably get it in the neck!
6. Even though the deadline for submitting expense budgets was clearly communicated in the e-mail, undoubtedly some departments will need to be manually followed up. Others will have been very prompt in returning their spreadsheets, but once they are opened in the finance department, it is clear that some of the data is missing and they need manually following up too.
7. After checking to ensure that all the spreadsheets have been returned, that the correct version has been used and that data is complete and has been entered against the right line items, finance can consolidate it all to produce the master budget spreadsheet. If everything goes well, consolidation will happen on the first attempt, driven by numerous formulas and macros. But if the macros break

or some clever departmental manager has inserted an extra row into their spreadsheet, the finance team will have to identify the problem, fix it and try again. Even then the only way to ensure that it has been successful is to run some manual checks.

8. But it is not finished yet. Many organizations make some charge backs for shared services and central expenses, and these costs will need to be calculated and apportioned back to the individual divisions or departments, typically requiring further re-keying by someone in the finance team. Then if they are lucky, they get some time off to do their Christmas shopping!

or similar solution. The automation of previously manual routines has dramatically improved productivity in many finance departments. Nor should one belittle the tremendous change in productivity that the advent of spreadsheets brought to the finance department. Anyone old enough to have used a slide rule at school and to have updated graphs with coloured pencils will testify to the transformation they have bought to business life. Spreadsheets are powerful and flexible tools for individuals who are modelling and analysing data on a desktop. They are just not that good for collecting and consolidating

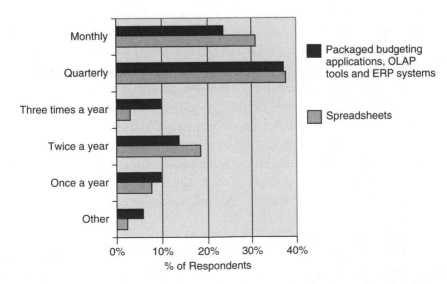

Figure 3.1 Comparison of the frequency of re-forecasts by the type of application used

expense budgets from hundreds of individual responsibility centre managers and have a number of well-documented shortcomings:

- It is difficult for budget controllers to keep track of various versions (e.g. budget, last re-forecast, latest iteration etc.), and budget contributors can easily rename and resubmit erroneous data. Operating with business critical information distributed around the company on spreadsheets is bound to result in problems. Somebody somewhere will be making business decisions from an old version of the budget. Is it their first submission, their last submission or the approved budget? Did they rename the file before they saved it away on their hard drive? There is simply no way of telling and already they are hiring up to the level they consider to be the approved budget.

- Spreadsheets are prone to errors. It has been estimated that 17% of spreadsheets contain errors. This implies that even the most diligent budget controller cannot expect 100% accuracy when consolidating individual spreadsheets from hundreds of budget contributors. They may be experts in writing macros, but something is likely to be amiss and more often than not they simply will not be aware of it as there is no way of identifying errors or omissions other than by doing an exhaustive manual reconciliation. In fact, moving to a packaged budgeting application where consolidation is automated often reveals these errors for the first time; the spreadsheet-based system simply never added up correctly and no one was ever aware of it.

- Spreadsheets do not have the inherent dimensionality needed for budgeting. Every single piece of data needed for budgeting has complex dimensionality. For instance, an expense amount is meaningless until it is associated with a line item such as "Salaries"; a department such as "Marketing"; a period such as "February"; a version such as "This Year's Latest Forecast"; perhaps a currency such as "Euros" and possibly other dimensions such as products, distribution channels and customers. Fitting this complex dimensionality into an inherently three-dimensional tool such as a spreadsheet with only Rows, Columns and Sheets to work with often means there has to be compromises. Typically this means limiting the amount of detail collected so that the management accountants can manipulate it and provide the various views of it required by different managers without having to do extensive reformatting or exhaustive re-keying.

- Spreadsheets have no formal audit trail so there is no way of knowing who last changed a cell value, when they did it and what the previous value was. Not only is this functionality important internally to preclude internal bickering, but it is rapidly becoming a prerequisite for good governance as boards are coming under increasing pressure to provide greater transparency into their future earnings. After 7 years of debate and discussion, in November 2005 the UK's Operating and Financial Review required directors of UK listed companies to provide guidance on factors likely to impact future profitability as part of their annual report was revoked by the Chancellor of the Exchequer. The derision and comment that erupted from those involved in drafting the legislation, the accountancy profession and from members of a number of FTSE 100 boards suggests that this piece of legislation will be resurrected and will eventually become law. However, a number of companies from among the FTSE 100 and many other not-for-profit organizations have already embraced the requirements of the Operating and Financial Review, some providing an extensive discussion of their future prospects in their annual report, their rationale being that their greater transparency will provide lenders and investors with confidence and lead to a lower cost of capital and more highly valued stock. So the debate may be temporarily on hold, but ultimately the budgeting process will need to be auditable and spreadsheets cannot provide this requirement. Spreadsheets were just never designed with rigorous financial controls in mind. They have no centrally administrated security making it virtually impossible to ensure that data has not been amended or viewed by individuals who do not have the authority. Attempts to limit access by using passwords or protecting portions of spreadsheets to preclude overwriting existing cell values are at best a desperate measure to build in some form of compliance. But all it tends to do is to add yet another layer of complexity and difficulty for both the finance department and the contributors. As long as they continue to use spreadsheets for planning and budgeting, companies will continue to face numerous compliance-related risks. In the current climate, their time is rapidly running out.

- Amending spreadsheets to include a new line item, a new product or an extra responsibility centre usually means a considerable amount of time and effort for someone in the finance department. It may involve making the same change to a large number of individual spreadsheets and it will almost certainly involve making changes to the formulas used for consolidating departmental expenses into the total company profit and loss account. Inevitably each amendment introduces an additional opportunity for error.

- Spreadsheets do not come with any workflow tools that help budget administrators manage and expedite the budgeting process. The typical

Case study: Issues with using spreadsheets for planning and budgeting

When Dale Hosack joined Western Container Corporation,[2] a Wisconsin-based manufacturer of wound paper tubes, cones and cans used in the food and beverage industry, he found a budgeting system that had not been updated for the last 20 years. But before he had time to gently implement a new system and mothball the old system, he was faced with a typical spreadsheet error that threw the company's financials into turmoil.

Western Containers' business is far from complex, just thirty customers and thirty products, so it was thought there was little need for a packaged budgeting application and for the last 20 years this US$350 million company had used one of the original spreadsheet packages for planning and budgeting. At the time the editors of *Business Performance Management* magazine interviewed Dale for an article published in their February 2006 edition, most organizations had long dumped this particular spreadsheet package and moved on to the ubiquitous package that people use today.

As an insider, Dale describes the budgeting process using spreadsheets as being very, very scary. Each of the manufacturing plants would send in their data in different formats, each spreadsheet having tabs for labour, raw materials and expense items. The central finance team had to roll them into a profit and loss account. During the annual budgeting process, the person responsible for this typically worked 12 hours a day for 6, and occasionally 7 days a week, burning the midnight oil to get the individual submissions into the format that finance required. When the original system was created back in 1984, the entire corporate budget fitted neatly into a single spreadsheet and the company only had one manufacturing plant. By the time Dale arrived that had grown into a monster with fifty-two tabs, some with formulas that linked and some with formulas that did not link. Whenever a new product was added, someone had to spend 3 days adding it into the tabs.

Dale knew he had to do something about the company's budgeting system as soon as he arrived, but he was overtaken by events. All too soon he found that a million dollars of expenses was missing from the consolidated profit and loss account; and as Western based their pricing on the expense forecast, it was also missing from the pricing. And how did this happen? Quite simply, one of the spreadsheet formula used to generate the consolidation profit and loss account had an error in it and no one had detected it.

Dale quickly rescued the situation and accelerated his plan to replace the spreadsheets with a packaged application that gave the finance department much better control of the process and alleviated many of the shortcomings of working with spreadsheets. But they have not gone away completely. Dale admits that down at the level where the people are really doing the budgeting work – the majority are doing it in spreadsheets, before clipping and pasting the data into the new budgeting system.

functionality of workflow tools includes being able to schedule e-mail alerts to contributor's mailboxes, having the ability to monitor how far individual contributors have progressed in submitting their budget or re-forecast, sending automated reminders of upcoming submission deadlines and, if absolutely necessary, timing out overdue contributions and using a prior version. As every cost centre submission usually involves the contributor who drafts the budget and their manager, who either accepts, amends or rejects it, and this may go through a number of iterations, workflow functionality is a definite advantage for administrators tasked with delivering a consolidated budget to a deadline. Increasingly, it is "must have" functionality for any enterprise planning and budgeting application.

Given that spreadsheets have these shortcomings when it comes to planning and budgeting inside large organizations, it is not surprising that those companies that used packaged budgeting applications gained some benefits. Table 3.2 shows the differences on a number of performance measures between companies using spreadsheets and companies using packaged planning and budgeting applications.

It is clear that moving to packaged planning and budgeting applications can help companies reduce the length of the annual budgeting cycle, and the survey results indicate the saving to be in the order of one week. The finance department in those companies using packaged applications will not have to burn the midnight oil and will have had a much easier time consolidating individual submissions into the final budget. However, the fact remains that the reduction in the time taken to produce the annual budget is modest. It is no more than a few days. When it comes to producing a re-forecast, the evidence

Table 3.2 Differences in elapsed time to produce budgets and re-forecasts between companies using spreadsheets and companies using packaged planning and budgeting applications

	Elapsed time to complete the annual budget	Elapsed time to complete a re-forecast
Companies using packaged planning and budgeting applications	12.4 weeks	2.52 weeks
Companies using spreadsheets	13.3 weeks	2.45 weeks

suggests there is little difference between companies using spreadsheets for planning and budgeting and those using packaged applications. In both cases, the findings suggest it is taking somewhere around twelve to thirteen working days, regardless of the application being used.

These findings suggest there is little difference in the performance measures for either annual budgeting or re-forecasting between those companies still using spreadsheets and those who have invested in packaged applications. The budget might contain fewer, previously undetected errors and the finance team might be having an easier time of it. There may even be an opportunity to reduce the headcount or redeploy resource elsewhere. But there is no evidence to suggest that packaged budgeting applications are allowing companies to re-forecast more frequently, and consequently these companies have no better visibility into their future than those still using spreadsheets. They have bought into the software vendors' marketing messages and made the investment in software licences and implementation services, but there is no evidence that these companies are any more agile than before. All this spending and little benefit; you have to ask, "Does anyone really understand what's going on here?" It is certainly more complicated than it first appears.

Corporate resistance to more frequent re-forecasting

There is a considerable amount of resistance to more frequent re-forecasting. In line with the findings of previous years, 97% of respondents surveyed during the most recent compilation of The Re-forecasting Survey reported that there were barriers to more frequent re-forecasts in their organization. The most frequent reasons mentioned are focused on two distinct areas: the line manager

Table 3.3 Barriers to more frequent forecasts

	Length of time it takes the finance department to manage a round of re-forecasting	Length of time it takes cost centre managers to review and resubmit re-forecasts	Line managers' resistance to more frequent re-forecasts
2002	26%	21%	16%
2003	25%	19%	14%
2004	15%	26%	26%
2005	23%	26%	19%

and the finance function. On one hand, respondents suggest that it takes line managers too long to review and re-forecast their line item expenses and they are resistant to suggestions of re-forecasting more frequently. On the other hand, respondents suggest that currently re-forecasting takes the finance department too long. The figures in Table 3.3 show that although there have been some fluctuation in the distribution of the responses, overall the level of resistance has not fallen during the 4 years in which the survey has been conducted.

These findings have implications for anyone considering introducing more frequent re-forecasting in their organization. The reported incidence of resistance from line managers suggests that adopting an incremental approach is likely to be the most successful with line managers able to experience the benefits of quarterly re-forecasts before moving to monthly re-forecasts. The findings also show the challenge of transforming the planning and budgeting process to reduce the amount of time cost centre managers need to review the re-forecasts.

Summary

Despite many organizations wanting to re-forecast more frequently and despite of an increasing proportion of organizations implementing packaged planning and budgeting applications, research shows that there has been little or no progress made in recent years. There is a logjam with planning, budgeting and re-forecasting with most organizations reporting resistance to more frequent re-forecasting. This is no to deny the undoubted benefits that many organizations have gained from abandoning spreadsheets as the main tool for budgeting and implementing packaged budgeting applications. They will have saved many hours preparing input schedules, consolidating individual submissions and manually checking and validating the results. This will have bought much needed efficiency to the budgeting process and improved productivity in the finance department. However, there is no evidence that the underlying process has changed as elapsed time taken to budget and re-forecast remains unchanged. Something more fundamental needs to be done.

Notes

1 The Re-forecasting Survey 2001–2005, available at www.algsoftware.com.
2 Excerpted and reprinted with permission, "Case in Point: The Pros of a Modern Budgeting Process", *Business Performance Management* magazine, February 2006.

4

The Limitations of
Traditional Budgeting

In the majority of organizations, the budget is the most important tool used to control performance. Senior managers might have spent time off-site working at clarifying their strategy under the guidance of an external consultant. The resulting strategy might be very sound and take account of all the likely external and internal issues that impact the organization's financial performance both in the short term and in the foreseeable future. It might have been translated into a success map in a balanced scorecard with appropriate measures and targets being cascaded down to individual managers. But when it gets to the wire, it is the budgeting process that takes precedent.

The budgeting process has received an increasing amount of criticism in recent years. As we have already seen in the previous chapter, it takes too long and therefore costs too much. But it has other shortcomings. Because of the rate of change in many markets, the annual budget is out of date almost before it is completed. That is why the ability to re-forecast more frequently is of such importance. Organizations need to routinely reassess the future and realign their operational plan and resources accordingly. Doing this once a year or even twice a year is not frequent enough for most organizations and they know it.

But critics of the budgeting process, most notably the Beyond Budgeting Round Table[1], also point to the effect that working with budgets has on people's behaviour. This has to do with the way budgets have come to be used today. The budgeting process fulfils a number of roles. Although it is managed by finance, budgeting is an enterprise-wide activity that some people suggest ought to be the responsibility of the chief operating officer. The argument is that the "planning" part of the "planning and budgeting" process is where strategy gets translated into actions and resource requirements, which are then assigned an anticipated expense. This is undoubtedly a critical role for budgeting and one which we shall return to later. But in most organizations the budget remains firmly in the control of the finance department. In companies where resources are limited, the budget is also a critical input into the cash flow statement and without it the entire future of the organization could be jeopardized.

Budgets and rewards

But with the rise of "management by objectives" and individual accountability during the 1960s and 1970s, accounting results such as income, return on capital employed and return on investment came to be used as targets for everyone from board members right down to departmental managers. This led to the budget becoming a critical determinant of many people's benefit and remuneration package. And when salaries, share options or pension contributions depend on beating the budget, there is everything to play for and everyone quickly learnt the rules of the game. Negotiating the fixed target typically begins with the senior members of the board establishing what is acceptable to their investors, bankers and analysts who follow their stock. Through a series of top–down and bottom–up iterations of the budget and individual negotiations, this target gets shared out between divisions until everyone knows exactly what their target is for the coming year. The rules of this performance contract are well known:

- Typically there is a fixed target for the financial year based on an absolute amount for sales or profits or a ratio such as the return on sales or return on capital.
- Individuals have a bonus plan based around the fixed target. In most organizations, there is a sliding scale that correlates the level of achievement with the amount of the bonus with payments starting for achieving just below the fixed target, rapidly increasing as the fixed target is achieved and then eventually reaching a plateau. In most companies, there is a published bonus scheme that clearly sets out the criteria for eligibility and details exactly how the scheme works with individual managers having a pre-determined monetary amount for an "on target" performance. However as one goes higher up the organizational structure, senior managers and board members are often able to negotiate their own performance contract.
- In their departmental or divisional budgets, managers will have agreed the resources needed to achieve the target both in terms of operating expenses and in terms of capital requirements.

Gaming with budgets

Having agreed the target and how people will be rewarded for achieving them, everyone involved with the organization ought to benefit from achieving it, including the investors and shareholders. But when there are such big rewards at stake, people are going to do everything possible to ensure they get them. Ultimately someone loses out and when it comes to rewards based on fixed targets, more often than not it is the investors and shareholders. There are a number of reasons for this, some more fundamental than others:

- Having been given an annual target, such as an absolute amount for profit, no one should be surprised when managers do everything in their power to ensure they achieve it. Typically this means padding out expense budgets and allowing for a good margin of safety with revenue projections.

The aim is to provide oneself or one's business unit with an easy target. To safeguard against senior management wanting to increase the target, managers "over-budget" and hide away contingency to accommodate their request. Alternatively, they have a raft of valid reasons why senior management's desire for increased profits fail to stand up to rigorous scrutiny. Either way they know they need to show some resistance, just in case senior management wises up to the gaming. Needless to say, the outcome of the negotiations is a target that is comfortable and managers need to ensure they achieve it, rather than significantly overachieve it, otherwise their credibility is blown and they will jeopardize the negotiation process for the following year. The target is certainly not a stretch target and neither is it in the best interest of the investors and shareholders.

- Because the target has an expiry date of the very last day of the financial year, anything that happens after that date is not an immediate concern. So having received a month-end finance report that shows things are beginning to drift and the chances of achieving the annual bonus are slowly slipping away, managers have some choices to make. First, they could reduce expenses for the remainder of the financial year. The danger here is that managers are left with insufficient resources to run their departments effectively, service levels start to suffer and once into the New Year, the business finds itself with a bigger problem of customer attrition. Or it could be that an important product development initiative is postponed for a few months. While it may have little impact on the business in the current year, managers may come to regret it if a competitor beats them to market next spring. Alternatively, managers could stuff the distribution channel offering customers an incentive to buy bulk before the end of the year. There is even a term for this practice, which is called "trade loading". Doing it will make this year's results look good, but the organization is in for a slow start to next financial year. None of these short-term actions is in the interests of stockholders and investors whose main concern is for the sustainable creation of value, rather than short-term fluctuations in earnings. Again they are losing out.

- Working towards annual targets encourages managers to keep both bad and good news hidden. As long as there is still time to correct any shortfall against the annual target during the coming months, managers tend to fudge their re-forecasts for fear of being admonished. Similarly if managers are aware of a significant slice of unbudgeted revenue that is about to come their way, they will tend to keep quiet for fear of being given additional sales quota. The result is no one quite knows the true picture. People game with their forecasts.

- Finally, when all the bad news does come to light and managers realize that there is no chance of earning any bonus, everyone may as well sacrifice the remainder of the current year to ensure they get off to a good start for the next financial year. They will continue to spend on whatever will bring future benefits as long as it can be put against this year's expenses and will do whatever they can to push sales into the next financial year. There may be strict rules in force for revenue recognition, but if contract negotiations are delayed for a few weeks so the revenue falls into the next financial year, no one will be any wiser, including the auditors.

In many instances, this type of behaviour is simply dysfunctional and never falls over into malpractice. But one can see how the relentless focus on achieving short-term targets and the temptation to conceal temporary shortfalls in earnings in the hope of them being made up later can quickly get out of control on the scale of Enron or Worldcom. One cannot blame the budgeting process per se for either the dysfunctional gaming of individual managers let alone the gross malpractice of senior executives. It is the foolhardiness of attaching financial incentives to its achievement that induces the dysfunctional behaviour. The literature suggests that organizations that have adopted a "beyond budgeting" approach to performance management still forecast their revenues and expenses using the same types of systems and processes that other companies use to generate budgets. The critical difference is that the output is no longer used as the basis for a fixed performance contract, for individual rewards and expenditure is not cast in stone for 12 months into the future.

Basing rewards on relative performance

If anything, the core idea of the Beyond Budgeting movement is that rewards should be based on the organization's performance relative to its peers rather than a pre-negotiated fixed target such as the annual budget. As such, organizations wishing to implement Beyond Budgeting need to start with the human resources function reshaping the remuneration and benefits policy, before the finance function can play its part by establishing more frequent re-forecasts and setting up comparative measures. Reading the literature produced by the Beyond Budgeting Round Table (BBRT) might lead one to believe that few companies ever benchmark their financial performance against their immediate competitors. This is clearly not the case. During their off-site strategy sessions, executives will have reviewed their growth and profitability against their competitors and increasingly companies exchange information in industry associations or purchase external data from organizations such as Hackett to benchmark their performance in specific areas of their business such as IT, finance and HR. What few companies have done is to base bonuses on comparisons with competitors.

A few of the companies that have happily adopted the Beyond Budgeting badge appear to have done it with the benefit of hindsight. Working with fixed targets never made sense in their particular market so they worked out other ways of rewarding people. For instance, it does not make sense for companies in the oil and petrochemicals industry to base rewards on a fixed performance target, such as the amount of annual profit, when oil prices are fluctuating widely. Shareholders in an oil company would not want to automatically pay out millions of dollars in performance bonuses when oil prices were rising, and conversely directors and managers would not want to automatically forego their bonuses when prices were falling. Many other sectors such as insurance, lending and capital equipment go through similar business cycles albeit not so dramatically.

What these companies have done is to base rewards on a group of high-level performance metrics that are compared with their industry peers, their prior year performance or some combination of both. This might include a weighted basket of measures such as return on capital employed and revenue growth compared to a selected peer group and compared to the previous year. There is no single approach, the only guidelines being that:

- Measures should be aligned with the company's strategy. If the strategy is to grow market share rapidly at the expense of short-term profitability, include a measure to reflect this and give it the highest weighting.
- Measures should be complementary rather than conflicting.
- Measures should be relative rather than absolute.

A consequence of adopting relative performance measures is that although the formula and basket of measures can be established well in advance of the financial year, relative performance can only be assessed once every company in the benchmarked peer group has published its results. This may mean delaying payment until well into the following year. An additional, but not insurmountable, complication may also arise when companies in the benchmarked peer group have different year ends. All that is needed is a formula for their published quarterly results to give a common year-end position.

What needs more consideration is exactly what to do when it is not possible to get meaningful data for comparison. This happens when one or more of the companies in the peer group operates in additional markets, territories or a distribution channel that you would prefer to exclude for comparison purposes and does not report these activities separately. Ultimately one has to decide whether to remove the company from the peer group, ignore the differing activities on the basis that they do not invalidate the fundamental comparison, which is typically at a very high level such as return on capital employed, or seek a proxy measure that one of the global benchmarking organizations can provide. Where it is still not possible to access viable data, the only alternative is to fall back on relative improvements over the previous year's performance.

Aligning rewards with the interests of investors

Using relative performance measures rather than a fixed performance contract as the basis for annual bonuses aligns the interests of executives and managers with those of investors and shareholders. Managers are no longer rewarded for their skills in negotiating targets and manipulating budgets. Neither will they get windfalls just because of some fortuitous event that no one could foresee when the budget was prepared. They will get rewards for improving their financial performance relative to their competitors and relative to their previous year's performance.

In many countries, and particularly in the US, boards are singularly focused on achieving their quarterly earnings figures in exactly the same way that managers are focused on achieving their annual targets. But while quarterly earnings are undoubtedly important, especially when they are way off expectations, they are not the be-all and end-all when it comes to creating value for shareholders. They want a financial return and this can only come from an increase in the value of their shares and the annual dividend payments. These need to be better than they could get by investing in other companies in the same industry sector, in other sectors, in other stock markets or by investing the money in other ways. Taking risk into account, they will buy shares in a company, effectively entrusting their money to the company's executives, if they can get a better return than they could get anywhere else. Modern theories of shareholder value suggest that in a perfect market, a share price reflects the net present value of the sum of future free cash flows and the value of the company's assets minus any debt. Future free cash flows include earnings, non-cash items and increases in working capital. This means that shareholders should not be solely concerned with short-term earnings or how much is paid as an annual dividend. Where the company is investing for the future, the size of future cash flows is equally, if not more, important. Witness the high prices investors are prepared to pay for stock in companies such as Google. The company may only generate modest profits today but it is investing heavily, it is in a growth market and the expectation is that future profits will be enormous. Their share price reflects this. Conversely, there are companies that compete in low growth markets, where a company with a high market share ought to enjoy higher profit margins and generate significantly greater free cash flows than a company with a lower market share. Again their stock price should reflect this.

So all that shareholders really want is a company to constantly grow future cash flows better than other companies in the market. As long as this is achieved, the share price should increase faster than that of competitors allowing investors to sell and take a profit whenever they wish. Fluctuations in short-term earnings only have any importance if they are interpreted as an early indicator of underlying problems such as a loss of market share, a slowdown in the market or an executive that is not fully in control of the business.

Theories of shareholder value have been around for 30 years or more and most chief executives and their CFOs will have encountered them in business school. So why have so few companies moved to bonus schemes based on relative measures? Is it because they and their managers will have less leeway to game their way to their annual bonus? Or, is it because adopting relative measures as the basis for bonuses means implementing another set of performance management tools such as the balanced scorecard to track and monitor performance? It would make a good topic for someone's doctorate.

Setting targets

Instead of relying on the annual budget as the roadmap against which to measure progress towards these relative objectives, companies need to implement other systems. Some of these objectives – such as "Move from the third quartile to the second quartile for return on capital employed by the end of the year", or "Grow revenue faster than any of the other top five companies in our market" – will be impossible to measure until all the necessary information about the competitors is made available in their annual reports or is available in a syndicated benchmarking survey. Yet no one can expect managers to maintain their focus and motivation unless they are provided with regular reports of how the company is progressing. This is easily done by establishing the objectives as high-level measures in a balanced scorecard and updating them whenever new information on the performance of companies in the benchmarked peer group becomes available. This is one instance where the practice of quarterly reporting does bring benefits. Competitors' results can be entered into the scorecard setting the benchmark against which to monitor progress.

Supporting these high-level objectives will be a set of other high-level performance indicators that are essential to monitoring progress and the successful implementation of the strategy. Where the board and executives have followed a systematic process to develop a strategy or success map that covers each of the traditional scorecard perspectives of financial, customer, internal processes and growth and learning, it is easy to identify the appropriate key performance indicators (KPIs). They almost reveal themselves. For instance, if one aspect of a company's strategy is to grow market share, then there are only two ways to do this; win more customers or sell more product to existing customers. Having followed this logic, it is apparent that suitable KPIs for the customer perspective might be a measure to reflect the number of active customers and a measure to reflect the average revenue per customer per period. Undoubtedly there would be other performance measures below these that are more specific to individual departments such as sales and marketing.

Neither the higher-level performance indicators nor the lower-level operational performance indicators form the basis of any incentive programme. But all of them directly contribute to the overriding goal of growing faster than the competition. It is this relative measure that is an element of the reward mechanism. Using scorecards rather than a budget to monitor performance has a number of benefits:

- Where the performance measures have been identified through a rigorous process of strategy development, perhaps using strategy or success maps, a scorecard will tell you whether the company is making progress in implementing its strategy and whether it is achieving the amount of profit it had projected for the current period. A monthly management report showing variances of revenues and expenses against budgeted numbers and simply tells you the latter.
- A scorecard that is founded upon a clear strategy and is systematically cascaded through the organization will help managers understand their priorities for implementing the strategy.
- Maintaining a reporting system for relative targets is quick and easy because they rarely change. For instance, a target such as moving into

the first quartile of one's peer group in terms of expense ratio will not need to be updated for some time. Short-term interim targets might be set in operational areas, but ultimately all that matters is continually monitoring that progress is being made. Inevitably this will mean internal comparisons of the current month's expense ratio against previous periods together with less frequent external comparisons against competitors. But none of this requires fixed targets to be set.

Executing strategy

In situations where strategy is not clearly defined or understood, the plans of individual departments and the assumptions they are based on can pull in different directions. At one extreme there will be some departments that strive for growth at all costs. At the other extreme there will be departments that will restrain resources and spending so that service suffers. Somewhere in the middle will be the majority. Typically without any particular focus, these departments will take the safe option and do what they have always done, which is to take last year's numbers and add a few percentage points. Needless to say, the resulting budget cannot be said to reflect a strategy.

Even in situations where there is a clear and well-communicated strategy and well thought–out action plans are developed and resourced to implement the strategy – an overly strict adherence to the annual budget will compromise execution. In many of today's markets, no one can possibly have the foresight to map out all their actions for the next 12 or 18 months. The business environment is simply too unpredictable. Yet in many organizations, departmental managers are expected to know exactly how they will use the expenses they have projected and submitting a departmental budget with unallocated amounts of money and contingencies is still frowned upon. Despite it being imperative to take advantage of a brief window of commercial opportunity or to counter an unanticipated problem, managers still struggle to get purchase orders for important resources authorised because they were "not budgeted for". Sometimes this rigidity can verge on the absurd such as when finance departments in cash-rich companies will not authorize purchase orders for resources prior to the period they were budgeted for and do not allow departmental managers to move expenses between line items, even though neither of these actions has any impact on the year-end position. These types of policies and an overtly strict adherence to the numbers in the annual budget limit agility at a time when business environments are increasingly unpredictable.

As long as the required resources are available and the company is not struggling for cash, any actions that work towards achieving long-term targets and maximize shareholder value should be welcomed. Faced with a request to provide funds for a new business initiative, all that the executive should ensure is that:

- The assumptions that underpin the request are sound and that any risks involved have been assessed and accounted for.
- The proposed actions are well-thought out and will help to achieve the long-term targets, such as improving the expense ratio or improving their ranking in the industry league tables in terms of return on capital employed.
- Any proposed capital spending has been through an appraisal process using a rigorous methodology such as discounted cash flow.
- There is currently no better way to use the required funds.

If the answers to all of these questions are positive, the funds should be made available and the resulting increase in revenues or reductions in expenses built into future re-forecasts. It is no longer the departmental manager who overspent who should be scrutinized. As long as there are appropriate procedures and approval levels in place for purchasing and capital expenditure, these managers are heroes and heroines. They know exactly what to do to create shareholder value. It is their colleagues who routinely end the year comfortably under-spent who should be scrutinized.

In many companies there will be quarterly meetings to review and approve requests for funding for new business initiatives. Rather than managing the business within the constraints of the annual budget, these companies have effectively turned themselves into more adaptive and agile enterprises where managers have access to funding as soon as they sense a competitive threat or a business opportunity. They know that throughout the financial year they can have access to funds as long as they prepare a business case ready for presenting to the quarterly strategy and review meeting. But if these meetings are to be effective and able to reach decisions quickly before the opportunity passes, they need access to reports from various performance management applications:

- A quick and easy way of forecasting how the initiative impacts revenues and expenses in future periods. For example, extending distribution into a new territory by appointing an overseas agent will grow revenues and increase expenses in future periods.

- Some way of accessing how the initiative impacts costs in future periods. Typically this is rudimentary and incomplete with many companies still approving large amounts of expenditure based on inadequate analysis. An increasing proportion of business expenses are indirect being incurred in shared service departments such as IT and HR that provide support to front-line departments or business units. This can mean that even seemingly straightforward initiatives such as re-engineering a business process can have complex implications on indirect costs that may be totally unforeseen. It is increasingly recognized that the only sure way to have robust and reliable unit costs for business processes, product costs and shared services costs is by implementing activity-based costing (ABC). Not only will this provide regular reports of unit costs which can populate the internal processes perspective of a scorecard and used to monitor progress towards both absolute and relative targets, it will also provide a practical tool for "what-if?" analysis incorporating the full inter-dependency of complex business relationships.
- A balanced scorecard that has linkages between low-level operational measures and the higher-level relative measures so that it is quick and easy to assess how the specific business initiative helps towards achieving the company's strategy and targets.
- A standardized methodology and agreed hurdle rates for approving capital expenditure.

Without these, discussion becomes subjective and decisions arbitrary, so that managers who are more skilful at arguing their case are more likely to receive funding regardless of the merits of their initiative.

Managing ongoing business processes

For ongoing business processes such as manufacturing products, answering calls in a contact centre or processing claims in an insurance company, there is neither the need for an annual budget nor the need to go through an approval process every time monthly expenses look set to increase. Monitoring expenses for ongoing business processes can easily be managed by setting departmental KPIs based on unit costs or expense ratios. Using unit costs, such as the cost to answer an inbound phone call or process a claim, is undoubtedly the best method particularly where unit costs are reported on a monthly basis and are generated through following an ABC methodology. Not only will these costs be accurate in that they will be "fully-laden" and incorporate the costs of the shared services that support the process, they will be generated by a consistent methodology making it easier to compare trends over time. As long as these unit costs are within acceptable parameters, or progress is being made towards a short-term target, there is little need to pay much attention to them. However, if there is a company-wide initiative to reduce total operating costs in order to close the gap between benchmarked competitors, managers can make use of the detailed information that ABC reporting generates to identify where to focus their attention. The imperative is no longer managing to the budget, but constantly seeking out opportunities to reduce unit costs.

Keeping a check on the cost of key business processes by monitoring expense ratios is a poor substitute in comparison with ABC reporting. Consider what practical insight you would gain from tracking a cost to income ratio such as the expense of running a contact centre against revenue. There is simply no way of telling whether an improvement in this measure was brought about by a change in the numerator or the denominator so that a simple increase in prices could easily mask an underlying increase in costs due to inattentive management. Activity-based costing wins every time.

Horizontal alignment

Implementing the balance scorecard to communicate strategy and make people accountable for its implementation will help achieve "vertical" alignment, but there remains the challenge of achieving "horizontal" alignment so there is little or no excess capacity anywhere in the organization.

At the time of preparing the annual budget, managers will actively work at aligning departmental resources regardless of what planning and budgeting system is being used. They will exchange information so that manufacturing capacity is in line with sales forecasts and call-handling capacity is sufficient to cope with the planned marketing activity. For that one moment, capacity will be aligned across the company; department by department and period by period. It is a masterpiece of careful coordination.

The tragedy is that all their careful work just gets turned into departmental line item expenses in the annual budget and within the first few months of the new financial year unanticipated changes in demand and unplanned actions in individual departments will have thrown everything out of line. What momentarily was in balance rapidly falls into disarray with some departments ending up under-resourced and others are over-resourced. Individual departments, such as contact centres, have tools to measure their productivity and utilization, but few companies have any enterprise-wide means of identifying areas of under- or over-capacity despite the damage that can result. In the short term the inability to fulfil orders or answer the telephone will make customers annoyed. In the long term, they could take their business elsewhere and recommend their family and friends to do the same. If this happens, the company's lack of focus on capacity management has destroyed shareholder value.

At the same time, excess capacity has a cost associated with it. Running a department with more resource than is actually required is a wasted expense and reduces profits. Either the excess capacity should be eradicated, put to use in another department or used for some other task that helps create shareholder value. Many companies have undertaken specific initiatives to reduce excess capacity, although these are usually limited to intra-departmental actions such as cross training customer service agents so they are able to deal with calls for two or more products. In instances like this, excess capacity is easy to measure and control, and where there is a pool of people willing to work limited hours, call centre managers can use call management software to schedule staff over busy parts of the day keeping resource tightly aligned with requirements. However, the standard monthly management report that simply compares actual expenditure against budgeted expenditure provides few insights to help anyone manage capacity. If the line item expense for salaries in a contact centre is 15% below budget, everything may look under control. But if the number of telephone calls answered is 20% below that assumed when the budget was prepared, there is probably excess capacity. Some of this might be justified in that it is always prudent to keep a buffer in readiness for when call volumes increase. But any capacity above this level is "idle" and reduces profits.

Monitoring expense ratios such as the cost of answering a call or processing an application draws management attention to excess capacity, but both the numerator (the line item expense) and the denominator (the number of calls or applications) still need to be monitored to understand the underlying causality. Ratios are useful indicators and any negative trends will soon set the alarm bells ringing. But other data is needed if companies are to optimize capacity across departmental barriers and it is simply not there in the traditional budget. At a time when it is increasingly difficult to accurately forecast revenues, capacity management is becoming more important and there are a number of ways companies can seek a solution. The most obvious remedy is to try to get the demand forecasting more accurate by forecasting at a greater level of detail and using sophisticated statistical forecasting techniques. Such endeavours undoubtedly help, but given the vagaries of many of today's markets, it may be foolish to place too much emphasis on extrapolating the past. A more fruitful approach might be to accept the inevitability that the revenue forecast will never be accurate and to strive to keep capacity aligned with demand.

In practice this means forecasting demand on a regular basis and building an enterprise-wide operational planning model that focuses on controllable costs. In many industries such as insurance the main controllable cost is staff and the operational planning model will be little more than a staffing model. In manufacturing industries, the controllable costs include other things such as inventory and stock.

Managing the business

Most managers rely more on these operational plans and staffing models than they do on the traditional budget and the monthly management accounts. Even if the finance department could provide departmental managers with their monthly accounts and variance reports at the stroke of midnight on the last day of the month, it is unlikely they would be any more useful. Most departmental managers will give them a cursory look, more interested in identifying any variances they were not anticipating than in seeking insight into those they already know about. Most management accounts simply confirm what departmental managers already know. For instance, if demand rocketed at the beginning of the month and temporary staff had to be brought in on higher wage rates to deal with it, it will come as no surprise that the line item for staff salaries is above budget. The manager knew that would happen the moment they telephoned the agency to request the staff. The finance department's rapid month-end reporting adds little value. What the departmental manager would really like is not "quicker history" but help in making better decisions about the future. A traditional budget contains little to help them do this as the budgeting process in most organizations involves the collection and consolidation of contributors' projections of the revenues and expenses they are responsible for. The process may include the collection of some non-financial data such as sales units, headcount or full-time equivalents (FTEs) but generally the focus of the exercise is line item expenses. To generate these, most contributors will typically work off-line on spreadsheets, first forecasting the demand on their department and then modelling the amount of resource required and the expense of that resource. In the study referred to in Chapter 3, respondents reported that their line managers use a variety of techniques to generate expense line item values. Of the respondents, 82% reported that their managers model part or all of their expense line items in spreadsheets; 17% reported that their managers model expense line items within the budgeting application itself; 4% reported using ABC software for high-level resource planning and 25% reported using simple estimation. Figure 4.1 shows how little this has changed during the 4 years that this survey has been conducted with only a small increase in the proportion of respondents reporting that their line managers did some modelling inside a packaged budgeting application.

In many instances, these techniques were used in tandem with one another. But the findings clearly show that modelling line item expenses in spreadsheets was almost a universal practice, with no discernable variance even in those instances where packaged budgeting applications were in use. Regardless of what application is used for budgeting, the majority of respondents recognized the importance of non-financial data when budgeting and re-forecasting. Over 30% of the respondents reported that non-financial data is used in the budgeting process and an increasing proportion of them expressed the desire to include non-financial data within the budget model alongside line item expenses. However for the moment, these off-line spreadsheets that contain

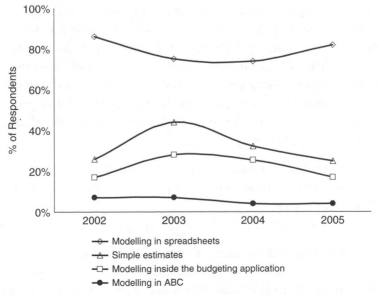

Figure 4.1 How cost centre managers generate their line item expenses

operational plans and staffing models are more important in managing the business than the budget, which in most instances contains little more than line item expenses. Perhaps this is why they are typically referred to as "working documents". When it comes to managing the business, they work; whereas a traditional budget no longer works.

The place of spreadsheets in business

It is worth reflecting on how spreadsheets fit into today's corporate environment at a time when organizations are coming under increasing legislation on compliance and corporate governance issues. Boards and executives are relying on budgets to provide analysts with guidance on future earnings. Increasingly they are also being pressured to be more transparent in their annual reports and provide guidance on how external and internal events are expected to impact their earnings in the future. This requirement was the focus of the UK's Operating and Financial Review, which was abandoned by the Chancellor of the Exchequer in the autumn of 2005. The unexpectedness of his announcement and the considerable criticism it provoked has led to discussion and consultations being restarted and the act looks set to be resurrected in the near future.

But in most companies there is a myriad of disparate spreadsheets underpinning the budget that are created and used by departmental managers to model resource requirements and line item expenses. These spreadsheets receive little attention from internal auditors and those responsible for risk management. They are often dismissed as "working papers", and are rarely recognized as being part of the formal budgeting process. But the reality is that they are the most important part of the planning and budgeting process. They may contain:

- Simple errors that result from manual re-keying.
- Hidden errors that arise when inexperienced spreadsheet users write and copy formulas.
- Erroneous assumptions about the external and internal environment.

A diligent management accountant may collect and review individual spreadsheets, checking to see that individual rows add up properly. But to go through an entire spreadsheet checking the formula in every cell is a major undertaking as is reconciling the output of one spreadsheet with the input of another. In most organizations it is unlikely to happen and even when it does it is unlikely to be thorough. It would take too long and cost too much.

So until legislation requires boards to provide guidance on future earning and the planning and budgeting process comes under the scrutiny of external auditors, most companies depend on a planning and budgeting process that is unreliable and far from robust. It is probably a good thing that most boards do not think about this too much. It is enough to make you break out in a cold sweat.

All too frequently finance departments send out budget schedules without providing contributors with any guidance on how they should go about filling it in. They might specify the date by when they want it returned to them. They might convey some expectations from the board about revenue growth and the target for the return on capital employed. But other than communicating these broad parameters, few finance departments offer contributors guidance on how to go about generating line item expenses for each period. All they ask is that you do – and that you send your completed submission back to them by the due date. This type of finance department sees budgeting primarily as a financial exercise. Some contributors also adopt the same approach simply adding on a few per cent to actual expenditure during the current year and submitting it as their budget. But thankfully many contributors involved in managing the day-to-day business know better. They hold the key to breaking the logjam in planning and budgeting.

Request a bottom–up, enterprise-wide re-forecast or next year's budget and most contributors will update and recalculate their resource planning spreadsheet, then re-key or "cut and paste" the resulting line item expenses into the enterprise budgeting application. Little wonder the annual budgeting process is so time-consuming and costly. The reality is that inside most organisations what is called the "budgeting process" has two distinct elements to it. First, line managers develop their operational or resource plan on a spreadsheet. This will include a forecast of the demand for each period, some fairly simple formulas to model the resources required and some forecast of unit resource costs to calculate certain of the line item expenses. Other line items will be simple estimates based on historic expenditure or "burn rates". If the manager is responsible for revenue, they will model things such as market size, market shares, sales volumes, selling prices and discounts. This is the "planning" part of the "planning and budgeting" process. Then when they are happy that their resource levels are aligned with demand and that their total expenditure matches up to any previously provided top–down guidelines on things such as salary awards and headcount, they will simply re-key or cut and paste their line item expenses into the enterprise budgeting application. This is the "budgeting" part of the process.

Some finance people and some software vendors simply talk about "budgeting" without acknowledging that in most instances it is a two-stage process: planning and budgeting. Some even talk about "budgeting and planning", metaphorically putting the cart before the horse and showing little understanding of what line managers are actually doing to generate line item expenses. It is impossible to budget without having first planned. This may seem a trivial point, but it is pivotal to transforming planning and budgeting. The failure to grasp the simple point that managers have to plan before they can budget is the reason why few companies that have implemented new packaged budgeting applications significantly reduce the length of their annual budgeting cycle or the time it takes to complete a re-forecast. All they have done is addressed the "budgeting" part of the process, leaving the "planning" part untouched.

It is evident that some finance departments have not considered the implications of this two-part process. This is clear from the type of questions that they ask in the requirement specifications that they send out to software vendors when shortlisting potential suppliers of budgeting solutions. For the most part, their questions reflect their concerns with making it easier and quicker for them to control and administer the budgeting part of the process. They will ask questions about version control, integration with general ledger systems and work management tools that will help them expedite budget submission and sign off. There is nothing wrong with this and implementing a new system will certainly make their lives easier and save some time and cost in the finance department.

Should any questions be included about functionality for contributors, they are usually limited to questions about functionality that accelerates data entry, such as spreading and "breakback". The latter of these is the very antithesis of integrated operational planning and budgeting. "Breakback" allows users to cascade a reduction in a consolidated number across a selected range of line item expenses. This functionality makes it very easy for the finance function to make large-scale adjustments to budgets when executives or their board of directors demand that expenses be cut; something that can be very common in the first iteration of a budget. It is achieved in a matter of minutes. But imagine the impact of this on a departmental manager who has diligently prepared an operational plan to forecast their resource requirements only to find their budget has been slashed. Their ability to implement what they intended is compromised and they are going to have to work with other departmental managers to develop a new operating plan where the expenses add up to the newly imposed target. It is back to those off-line spreadsheets to make some trade-offs. Is it any wonder that departmental managers pad out their expense forecasts with contingencies? They anticipate these types of imposed cuts and ensure that they are able to accommodate them without having to rework their operating plans. Given the circumstances, this can hardly be called "gaming". It is what anyone who really understands that there are two distinct parts to planning and budgeting would do. These managers are smart; "breakback" certainly isn't!

The traditional budget that only collects and consolidates line items expenses offers little facility for testing different assumptions and scenario planning. Try as you might, there is no possible way it can provide any insight into how profitability might be effected should your customer attrition rate increase or one of your key accounts desert you mid-year. It is a set of "dumb" numbers. The only way to test assumptions is by going back to each departmental manager and asking them to rework their individual operating plans to see how their departmental expenses change and then re-consolidating the budget to provide an enterprise-wide view. This will take time because departments such as production and logistics that are downstream of sales and marketing cannot make any changes until the new sales volumes and revenues have been re-forecast. The findings from the survey referred to in Chapter 3 suggests a single iteration will take somewhere around 12 working days. This means that detailed bottom–up scenario planning and fine-tuning budgets and operating plans to align capacity across the organization is rarely if ever achieved.

Traditional budgets are little more than a collection and consolidation of "dumb" numbers. Finance departments can provide monthly management accounts showing variances between actual expenditure and budgeted expenditure. If their expenditure is below plan, cost centre managers will be happy; if it is above plan, cost centre managers will be sad. But month-end expense reports add little to anyone's understanding of exactly what is happening in the business or what might happen in future periods. The real insight lays elsewhere hidden away on a myriad of disparate operational plans on departmental managers' desktops. Until we have fully appreciated that budgeting cannot happen without planning, we will never transform the process into something that can support businesses in today's uncertain markets.

Summary

Any budget controller who is dissatisfied with their current budgeting process may well be confused about how to go about making it better. On the surface, the BBRT seems to be suggesting that organizations should abandon budgeting completely. However once you dig into the detail, their main premise is that rewards and bonuses should not be tied in to the achievement of an annual fixed budget. As such many of important ideas that underpin Beyond Budgeting are not the concern of the finance function at all and really belong to the board and the human resources department. In practice, many of the organizations cited in BBRT case material still operate with rolling re-forecasts and flexible resource plans, which most finance people would recognize as a budget in anything but name.

Linking rewards to relative measures such as improvements over the previous year or outperforming industry peers will encourage organizations to become much more dynamic and responsive to internal and exchanges changes and to continually seek out opportunities that create value. This will force them to abandon annual fixed budgets and work towards managing with more frequent rolling re-forecasts. However, unless they integrate planning and budgeting into a seamless process, organization are unlikely to be able to re-forecast with the frequency they desire, no matter how they want to reward their staff.

Note

1 The manifesto of the BBRT is set out in "Beyond Budgeting", by Jeremy Hope and Robin Fraser, Harvard Business School Press, 2003, ISBN 1–57851–866–0.

Driver-Based Budgeting

The traditional budgeting process is hierarchical and focuses on collecting and consolidating individual contributions to produce the enterprise profit and loss account. But when managers generate their departmental budgets, they are modelling the operational drivers and causal relationships that run horizontally across an organization. When asked to produce a budget or a re-forecast, the managers' first concern is that the department upstream of them provides them with a reliable forecast of future demand. In fact, until they have received this, they cannot start their own departmental planning.

Consider the manager of a large call centre responsible for a team of telemarketing staff, taking inbound telephone enquiries from homeowners seeking property insurance. First, he needs the marketing department to provide him with a forecast of the number of inbound enquiries for each of the coming months. Then, by modelling resource consumption rates and unit resource costs, he can forecast his line item expenses for staff costs. At the same time, by modelling the sales conversion rate, he can provide the underwriting department downstream of him with a forecast of the number of new policy applications they will have to process.

The worked example in Table 5.1 shows how driver volumes, consumption rates, unit resources costs and other assumptions are modelled to generate the line item expense for staff costs in the call centre that is the central department in Figure 5.1.

If the above example was in an organization using traditional budgets, the three managers involved would have had to exchange information, typically sending

Table 5.1 Example of modelling operational drivers to generate line item expenses

Input from marketing	# Inbound enquiries this month	80,000	
Modelling of line item expenses in the call centre	# Working days this month	20	
	# Calls per agent per day	50	
	# Agents required	80	80,000/(20×50)
	Allow 10% to handle peaks/absences	88	80+10%
	Average Cost (£) per agent per month	1,500	
	Staff cost (£)	132,000	88×1,500
Output to underwriting	Sales conversion rate (%)	16	
	# New policy applications	12,800	80,000 × 16%

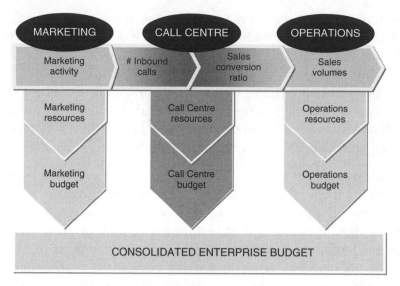

Figure 5.1 Example of inter-departmental drivers running across a business

their entire spreadsheet to their colleagues next in the process. Then they would have to work through an unfamiliar spreadsheet to isolate the pieces of information they require and re-key or cut and paste it into their own spreadsheet to model their own resource requirements and generate their department's line item expenses. All of this takes time and introduces the risk of errors.

What is a driver?

Driver-based budgeting uses both non-financial and financial driver data to model line item expenses. Drivers will differ by industry and even by company and it might appear as though there is no hard and fast definition of what makes a driver. But if we think about the types of drivers that have been used in the above example and how they were used, we can establish a working definition:

In driver-based planning and budgeting, a driver is a piece of non-financial or financial data which when changed directly impacts either revenues or expenses, ultimately changing the forecast profit and loss account, cash flow and balance sheet.

There are some points you should note in this definition:

- It starts by saying, "In driver-based planning and budgeting". This is because the term "driver" is used for assigning expenses to activities and activity costs to cost objects in ABC. As we will see later, many of the drivers an organization would use for planning and budgeting are identical to those they would use for cost assignments in ABC. Many drivers would also be important metrics to monitor in a scorecard. But for the moment, let us limit ourselves to driver-based planning and budgeting.

- The definition limits drivers to those things, which directly impact either revenues or expenses. This means they can be included in a rule or formula that will directly calculate either a revenue figure or a line item expense. What we are not including here is more intangible concepts such as customer satisfaction which some researchers have found to correlate with overall profitability, but which cannot be used to calculate detailed revenues or line item expenses.

Different types of driver

If we use the above definition to restrict our attention to factors that directly impact revenues or line item expenses, we see there are many different types of drivers that are used in planning and budgeting. These include the following:

Quantitative measures of demand

This includes both the forecast level of demand for the products or services sold to customers and the level of demand faced by individual departments.

Examples:

- Market size and market share
- The number of sales units of a product
- The number of inbound telephone calls
- The number of late payments to follow up
- The number of active customers
- The number of items per sales order
- The number of pieces of direct mail sent to prospects.

Consumption rates, productivity rates or cycle times

These measure the amount of resource required to satisfy demand or produce a unit of output.

Examples:

- Simple productivity ratios, such as the number of calls per agent per day – as used in the example above
- Cycle times, such as the average duration of a call
- The amount of space needed by each full-time equivalent (used to model the facilities requirement)
- The ratio of staff to supervisors.

Unit resource costs

The average cost of a unit of resource during a period.

Examples:

- The cost of a litre of fuel
- The average salary cost of a particular grade of staff
- The anticipated cost of replacing a desktop computer.

Unit selling prices

The average selling price of a product or service.

Examples:

- The average premium of a particular type of insurance policy
- The anticipated fee for each consulting engagement
- The anticipated selling price for a particular product.

Other drivers used in modelling

In addition to the types of driver listed above, there will be a host of other arithmetic functions used to model revenues and expenses. Many of these drivers will be probabilities and percentages such as:

- The proportion of inbound telephone calls that result in a sale.
- The anticipated rate of customer attrition, which may be used to model the number of active customers and subsequently forecast the anticipated revenue.
- The probability of policyholders making a claim on their insurance policy.
- The proportion of new sales orders that get invoiced during the current month.

Many of these probabilities and percentages can be measured and monitored by taking data from transaction processing systems. For instance, many organizations will already be routinely measuring their customer attrition rate and insurers will be constantly monitoring claims frequency as one of their key performance indicators. However, we should not delude ourselves that every element that goes into a driver-based planning and budgeting model is based on accurate measurement. Some elements will be little more than rules of thumb; simple assumptions that departmental managers have used when forecasting their line item expenses. For instance, in the example above, the contact centre manager included a 10% buffer in the number of staff to allow for training and one-to-one coaching, holidays and absences as well as some excess capacity to handle peaks. Who is to know if this assumption is correct? When building a driver-based planning and budgeting model from scratch, it is best to start off by accepting such a figure without too much argument. But after a few months of actual data, it will rapidly become clear from comparing the actual staffing against the modelled requirement whether 10% is the right figure to use or whether it should be changed. Driver-based planning and budgeting surfaces many of the assumptions and rules of thumb that individual managers routinely use in forecasting line item expenses. But getting them out into the open means they can be easily monitored and refined, keeping line item expenses more aligned with changing levels of demand.

So although some of the data elements that go into a driver-based planning and budgeting model may not be hard and fast numbers or monetary amounts, and some of them may start off as assumptions, they are all "drivers" in that if when they are changed, either revenues or line item expenses are directly impacted.

Characteristics of drivers

Drivers also differ according to where they are used in the model:

Intra-departmental drivers

Some drivers are only important in one department. For instance, the drivers involved in forecasting staffing requirements and salary expenses in a contact centre are only important to the department manager and their superior. In a driver-based budgeting model, this will be a simple rule that is restricted to this department, but applies to all periods and versions.

Inter-departmental drivers

Many drivers run horizontally across organizations, spanning departments just like the business processes they are part of. The output of one department becomes the input of other departments downstream from them. In certain instances, this may be a one-to-one relationship such as between the contact centre and the underwriting department in the example above. In other instances, such as when a new sales forecast is produced, it will be a one-to-many relationship with virtually every department needing to re-forecast.

The rule needed to do this is no more complex than that needed for an intra-department rule. It is just that the output of the rule becomes the input for a number of other departments. What is important is that these downstream departments are quickly alerted that they need to re-forecast themselves and that they have immediate access to the new data. Most vendors or packaged budgeting applications provide a work management tool that allows the budget administrator to pre-schedule standard routines that will expedite preparing and authorizing budgets and re-forecasts. These can be configured to automatically alert a contributor that the department upstream of them has completed a new submission and it is now their turn to review and re-forecast their expenses. This takes care of the first requirement.

But not all vendors can address the second issue of providing immediate access to the new data. This is because their software only provides individual contributors with a download of their departmental model as a subset of the overall model. They can take their departmental model and work off-line to review and re-forecast their department. But before any of their changes are available to a downstream department, the whole model has to be re-consolidated, recalculated and re-distributed to the next department in line. Doing this once during the annual budgeting process or monthly re-forecasting process might be possible but doing it numerous times to accommodate a whole series of changes across a string of interlinked departments is impractical. Systems requirements for driver-based planning and budgeting are discussed in detail in Chapter 9.

Drivers that span time periods

Some drivers span time periods. This happens when an event in one period has impacts in one or more periods in the future. A simple example of this is where sales orders or new business applications received during one calendar month are not fulfilled until the following month. For instance, if it takes ten working days to fulfil a sales order, approximately half of the orders received during a particular calendar month will not be fulfilled until the following month. A quick analysis of the historic pattern of the volumes of sales orders and completed shipments will soon reveal a relationship that can be used as a rule in a planning and budgeting model. In the example in Table 5.1, not all of the forecasted 12 800 new policy applications will arrive in the underwriting department in the current month; a third of the initial sales made in the current month arrive in the underwriting department in the following month. Therefore, when the manager of underwriting is doing his resource modelling, he may need to split the 12,800 applications between the current month and the following month in the ratio 2:1.

Similarly many other key drivers of financial performance, such as customer attrition rate, need modelling over time periods in order to forecast future demand and ultimately financial performance. Most organizations working in financial services, such as general insurance where there are large numbers of policyholders paying monthly premiums, will have developed sophisticated customer retention models that measure the separate elements of mid-term cancellations and policy renewals. By monitoring these every period, these companies are able to build predictive models that can quickly forecast the number of active customers in future periods. Multiplying the number of active customers by the forecasted average premium for the month when they are due to renew their policy forecasts the written premium. In the example shown in Table 5.2, an insurer has 100 000 active policyholders who renewed their policy in January paying an average monthly premium of £15. The insurer has a monthly mid-term cancellation rate of 0.75% and a policy renewal rate of 80%.

By the end of the first policy year there are only 91,362 active policyholders who can be invited to renew their policy. Of these, 80% renew their policy at the higher premium of £16 each month, and then they steadily dwindle at the same mid-term cancellation rate of 0.75%. For simplicity, the mid-term cancellation rate has been kept static at 0.75%, although many insurers will have sophisticated business intelligence tools that allow them to measure this each period. You should also note that the premiums have only been modelled for those customers whose policy year runs from January to December and to complete the premium forecast all the other policyholders whose policies

Table 5.2 Example of customer retention and policy renewal modelling

	January	February	March	April	May	June	July	August	September	October	November	December
Year 1												
Number of active policyholders at start of month	100,000	99,250	98,506	97,767	97,034	96,306	95,584	94,867	94,155	93,449	92,748	92,053
Mid-term cancellation rate (%)	0.75	0.75	0.75	0.75	0.75	0.75	0.75	0.75	0.75	0.75	0.75	0.75
Number of active policyholders at end of month	99,250	98,506	97,767	97,034	96,306	95,584	94,867	94,155	93,449	92,748	92,053	91,362
Average number of active policyholders during the month	99,625	98,878	98,136	97,400	96,670	95,945	95,225	94,511	93,802	93,099	92,400	91,707
Average monthly premium (£)	15	15	15	15	15	15	15	15	15	15	15	15
Written premium from these policyholders (£)	1,494,375	1,483,167	1,472,043	1,461,003	1,450,046	1,439,170	1,428,376	1,417,664	1,407,031	1,396,478	1,386,005	1,375,610

Year 2

Number of policyholders invited to renew their policy	91,362										
Renewal rate (%)	80										
Number of active policyholders at start of month	73,090	72,542	71,997	71,457	70,922	70,390	69,862	69,338	68,818	68,302	67,789	67,281
Mid-term cancellation rate (%)	0.75	0.75	0.75	0.75	0.75	0.75	0.75	0.75	0.75	0.75	0.75	0.75
Number of active policyholders at end of month	72,542	71,997	71,457	70,922	70,390	69,862	69,338	68,818	68,302	67,789	67,281	66,776
Average number of active policyholders during the month	72,816	72,269	71,727	71,190	70,656	70,126	69,600	69,078	68,560	68,045	67,535	67,029
Average monthly premium (£)	16	16	16	16	16	16	16	16	16	16	16	16
Written premium from these policyholders (£)	1,165,050	1,156,312	1,147,640	1,139,032	1,130,490	1,122,011	1,113,596	1,105,244	1,096,954	1,088,727	1,080,562	1,072,458

start during the months February to December would have to be modelled. But change any number during any period and the written premium will be affected for many months into the future. Table 5.3 shows what happens if the policy renewal rate falls to 70% and the monthly mid-term cancellation rate increases to 1%.

The net effect of these changes is that there are over 10,000 less active policyholders left in December of Year 2 and one can only hope there is sufficient new business being written to make up for this. In essence, this model is using the "leading" indicators of monthly mid-term cancellation rate and annual renewal rate to predict the "lagging" written premium. Adopting this approach will inevitably lead towards rolling re-forecasts as organizations realize the superficiality of the traditional 12-month planning and budgeting timescale. It is also apparent that these and many other non-financial drivers that are used in driver-based budgeting are also likely to be important measures in the customer perspective of any scorecard. Not only do these drivers need to be constantly monitored. As soon as any deviation from a steady state is detected, the likely impact on future financial performance needs to be rapidly assessed. That can only be done with a driver-based budgeting model.

Most driver-based planning and budgeting models start from some measure of demand. In consumer markets, this might be a market-based model with market size, market growth and market share being the drivers of sales volumes and demand across the entire model. Organization competing in business-to-business markets might start by using the amount of sales and marketing activity as the primary driver of demand for their model. But it is wrong to assume that all driver-based planning and budgeting models need to start with a measure of demand as their primary input. In certain manufacturing and supply industries, plant and assets have to be in continuous use around the clock if the organization is to be commercially viable. In such situations, production capacity has to be the primary input into any driver-based model with most other resources being driven by the need to produce and sell the output for the highest possible price. In Figure 5.2, this type of model is called Asset Based or Capacity Based. Again there is generally little need to deliberate over which type of model best fits the organization. Most will have iteratively worked out the way their business works and will already be using an appropriate methodology to model revenues and resource requirements. All finance need to do is integrate these models into the budgeting process.

Table 5.3 Revised example of customer retention and policy renewal modelling

	January	February	March	April	May	June	July	August	September	October	November	December
Year 1												
Number of active policyholders at start of month	100,000	99,000	98,010	97,030	96,060	95,099	94,148	93,207	92,274	91,352	90,438	89,534
Mid term cancellation rate	1.00%	1.00%	1.00%	1.00%	1.00%	1.00%	1.00%	1.00%	1.00%	1.00%	1.00%	1.00%
Number of active policy holders at end of month	99,000	98,010	97,030	96,060	95,099	94,148	93,207	92,274	91,352	90,438	89,534	88,638
Average number of active policyholders during the month	99,500	98,505	97,520	96,545	95,579	94,624	93,677	92,741	91,813	90,895	89,986	89,086
Average monthly premium	£15	£15	£15	£15	£15	£15	£15	£15	£15	£15	£15	£15
Written premium from these policyholders	£1,492,500	£1,477,575	£1,462,799	£1,448,171	£1,433,690	£1,419,353	£1,405,159	£1,391,108	£1,377,196	£1,363,424	£1,349,790	£1,336,292

(continued)

Table 5.3 (Continued)

	January	February	March	April	May	June	July	August	September	October	November	December
Year 2												
Number of policy holders invited to renew their policy	88,638											
Renewal rate	70%											
Number of active policyholders at start of month	62,047	61,426	60,812	60,204	59,602	59,006	58,416	57,832	57,253	56,681	56,114	55,553
Mid term cancellation rate	1.00%	1.00%	1.00%	1.00%	1.00%	1.00%	1.00%	1.00%	1.00%	1.00%	1.00%	1.00%
Number of active policy holders at end of month	61,426	60,812	60,204	59,602	59,006	58,416	57,832	57,253	56,681	56,114	55,553	54,997
Average number of active policyholders during the month	61,737	61,119	60,508	59,903	59,304	58,711	58,124	57,543	56,967	56,398	55,834	55,275
Average monthly premium	£16	£16	£16	£16	£16	£16	£16	£16	£16	£16	£16	£16
Written premium from these policyholders	£987,787	£977,909	£968,130	£958,449	£948,865	£939,376	£929,982	£920,682	£911,475	£902,361	£893,337	£884,404

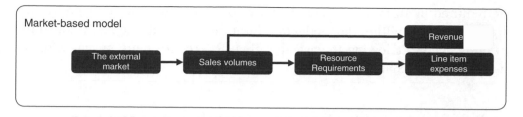

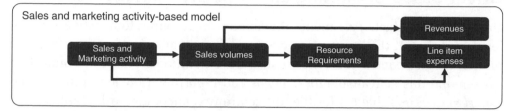

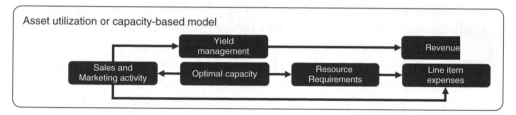

Figure 5.2 Types of driver-based planning and budgeting model

Driver-based budgeting and fixed costs

Most of the focus of driver-based planning and budgeting is on variable or controllable costs, predicting line item expenses such as salary, raw materials, postage and telephony. However, many so-called "variable costs" are in effect "step-fixed". For instance, a driver-based budgeting model may suggest that 88.5 FTEs are required to handle the forecast number of inbound calls. You cannot have 88.5 full-time staff and the only way to satisfy this level of resource requirement is by combining a fixed element of permanent staff with a variable element of overtime. Alternatively, you could decide to employ 86 permanent employees and run with a small margin of excess capacity.

Other fixed expenses, such as property costs and depreciation costs for equipment, can also be modelled. For instance, property costs are typically classified as fixed. However, over the time horizon of a re-forecast they may need to be considered as variable. For example, if our call centre can only accommodate 100 seats and our budgeting model suggests more than a hundred agents will be required in 16 months' time, we need to know. This can be done by configuring an alert within the model to inform the user that a capacity constraint is approaching, allowing them ample time to procure more space, with the associated step change in costs.

Driver-based budgeting and capacity management

Driver-based budgets first model the amount of resource to satisfy a forecast level of demand, then cost it to generate a line item expense. Therefore, the model contains considerably more data than is traditionally held in a budgeting system and this is available for analysis and reporting. Consider a month-end report shown in Table 5.4 for the call centre first encountered in Table 5.1.

With a traditional budgeting system that contains little but line item expenses, the only thing visible is the salary costs for the contact centre which are 6.25% above plan. Any diligent management accountant would set out to seek an explanation for this overspend from the departmental manager. But in a driver-based budgeting system, the higher volume of inbound calls which was 10.5% above plan is reported. In fact the call centre team performed exceedingly well – they raised productivity by 4% – and limited the amount of overspend. In this scenario, anyone reading the report does not simply know that something has happened; they know exactly why it happened! Any management accountant

Table 5.4 Variance reporting in driver-based budgeting and traditional budgeting

	Driver-based budget			Traditional Budget		
	Plan	Actual	Variance (%)	Plan	Actual	Variance (%)
# Inbound enquiries	80,000	88,400	+10.5			
# Workings days	20	20	–			
# Calls per agent per day	50	52	+4			
# Agents required	80	85	+6.3			
Average salary cost per agent	£1,500	£1,500	–			
Salary expenses	£120,000	£127,500	+6.25	£120,000	£127,500	+6.25

confronting the contact centre manager without this information would surely get short shrift.

Knowing that the expenses for a responsibility centre are above or below plan is incomplete information. Until we know more we cannot take any action. However, if we have access to information about the level of demand facing that responsibility centre during the period, the amount of resource required to satisfy that level of demand and the amount of resource actually provided, we know exactly what action to take. We can immediately see where excess capacity exists and take action to bring it into line with what is actually required. At a time when profitable revenue growth is increasingly difficult to achieve, keeping resources tightly aligned with trading is a problem common to many sectors. Sometimes called "consumption-based" planning and budgeting or "resource consumption analysis", the above approach demonstrates the key characteristics of driver-based planning and budgeting: it is all about building a dynamic budget where drivers are used to model revenues and line item expenses within the planning and budgeting application.

Driver-based budgeting vs. activity-based budgeting

Although there are considerable similarities, driver-based budgeting is not the same as activity-based budgeting (ABB). Activity-based budgeting, as described in numerous publications and papers[1], relies on detailed cost decomposition and the prior existence of an ABC model.

Activity-based costing methodology has been around since the early 1980s and has been in and out of fashion a number of times before steadily gaining more widespread adoption in recent years. Companies have realized that despite the large amounts they have invested in new transaction systems, data warehouses and customer relationship management systems, they still have little reliable data about the profitability of their products, customers and marketing channels or the cost of various business processes. Many of the earlier ABC implementations went into too much detail with many hundreds, and sometimes many thousands, of separate activities. When analysis was done at this level, a lot of non-system data needed to be collected about how departments split their time across the various activities they performed. It was laborious, time-consuming and costly to collect and collate this data. This led to infrequent reporting and inevitably many implementations simply withered away.

Unlike many management fads, ABC refused to die though. There has never been anything to take its place and probably never will be. This is because the make up of the cost base has changed substantially over the last 30 years or so with a proportionate decline in direct costs and an increase in indirect costs such as technology and sales and marketing. At the same time the creation of both products and services has become more complex and the importance of customer service functions has increased. As a result of these changes, overheads and indirect costs form a much more significant part of corporate expenditure in all industries and there needs to be some way of assigning these expenses to products, customers and channels. This is the role ABC fulfils today. Without it, how else do you know how to price products accurately, which customer segment to focus on to optimize profits, or how to reliably allocate IT charge outs to business units?

Activity-based costing may have received bad press in the past, mainly due to overzealous practitioners getting overwhelmed by the methodology. But today, the focus is firmly on providing business users with insight about costs and profitability so they can make better-informed decisions. As a result of this, models have tended to be less detailed with the emphasis has been on providing a larger number of users with more frequent reports. At the same time, the advent of web-based ABC applications has removed much of the drudgery and cost involved in collecting non-system data and reporting. This has substantially reduced the cost of doing ABC and enabled leading-edge companies to provide monthly ABC reports at the same time as part of their monthly management pack.

So although ABC is often assumed to be complex and consequently may seem rather impenetrable, this is something of a misconception. Although the various assignments of cost can be hard to unravel this is usually handled by software tools, while the methodology itself actually stems from a few basic principles, which are really just common sense.

Principle 1: Activities consume resources

Companies employ people and use resources to carry out activities. The more an activity is performed, the more resources it will consume.

Principle 2: Activities have causes

All activities are performed for a reason or a cause. Most activities are attributed to external objects such as customers, products or distribution channels, although some activities – such as those in IT and HR departments – will have an internal cause, such as the demand from the organization's front-line departments. Activities may be classified according to whether they are value-adding or non-value adding, the latter being activities such as rework and resolving customer complaints.

Principle 3: Different customers, products and channels cause different levels of activity

Traditional costing methods, such as standard costing or absorption costing, allocate base costs directly to products, customers and distributions channels. These methods ignore the principle that resources are actually consumed by activities, and not by products, customers or channels. Having first assigned expenses to activities, ABC allocates costs to customers, products and channels in line with the activities they actually consume. Table 5.5 lists the common terms used in ABC and if you wish to brush up on your understanding of the basic ABC methodology, you can find a worked example in Appendix 2.

It is unlikely that all the resource cost would ever be allocated to activities. Some resources such as sales and marketing expenses can be directly attributable to specific groups of customers or products and it makes little

Table 5.5   Definitions of common ABC terms

Term	Definition	Example
Resource	A facility, asset or other means used by the company to carry out its business	Staff costs, property costs, assets, capital, operating costs
Resource driver	A measurable quantity used to allocate resources to activities	Headcount, time spent, floor area
Activity	A series of tasks that are carried out repeatedly	Do a credit check; retool a milling machine; dispatch an order
Activity driver	An event or factor that causes activity to be performed	Invoices sent to customers
Cost objects	The entities that are to be costed	Customers, products, distribution channels

sense to take these through activities. These are specific to particular cost objects and can be assigned directly to those cost objects. In other instances, defining a causal link to customers and products is far from obvious and may not be meaningful. For example, most of the activities carried out by a company's CEO would probably not be attributable to particular products or customers. These non-specific costs can either be excluded from the model altogether or reassigned to all other activities. Figure 5.3 shows the flow of costs in ABC.

Both driver-based budgeting and activity-based costing include the word "driver" in their lexicography, and no doubt this has led to people assuming that driver-based budgeting and ABB are one and same thing. They are definitely not. Many of the resource drivers and activity drivers used in activity-based costing model or an activity-based budget will be identical to those used to develop a driver-based budget. For example, in Appendix 2, there is a simple worked example of activity-based costing, using an activity cycle time as a driver. If this organization were building a driver-based budget, most likely the same driver would be used in a rule to calculate the resource requirements and line item expenses for the department.

Changing driver volumes and "back-calculating" an ABC model produces a revised set of line item expenses. If each line item is set as either a variable

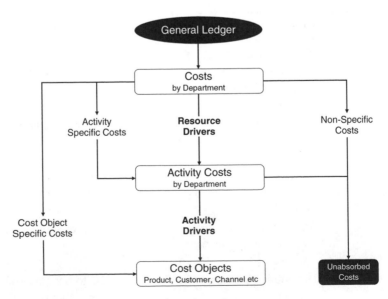

Figure 5.3 The flow of costs in activity-based costing

expense or a fixed expense, and known capacity constraints are identified, the resulting expenses will be fairly accurate. In fact they are likely to be more accurate than those that are the result of a traditional budgeting process with its protracted negotiations over a number of iterations. Activity-based budgeting removes all the gaming and ensures that all discussions about the budget are based on fact.

Until recently few ABC applications were capable of handling multiple periods and the very nature of cost decomposition through a structured ABC approach meant that ABB was overly deterministic. Some of the new generation of ABC applications allow for multiple periods and let users incorporate user-defined rules into the ABB calculation. This allows users to better reflect reality in their ABB model such as the fact that activities occurring in one period have an impact in a subsequent period or that in real life an increased level of activity may be resourced in a different way. For instance, a user-defined rule might calculate that as long as the increase in the amount of activity in a particular department is less than a certain percentage and does not persist for more than a single period, it will be resourced with full-time staff by paying them overtime at the hourly rate of "time and a half"; otherwise it will be resourced by recruiting additional full-time staff at the standard hourly rate. Similarly a user might decide to change some of the activity drivers or resource drivers in any future period to reflect anticipated changes in productivity or changes in business processes. But ultimately, ABB can be as simple as reversing the most recent relationships in an ABC model.

The Consortium for Advanced Management, International (CAM-I) has developed the most comprehensive model of ABB; resulting in its publication "The Closed Loop" authored by Stephen Hansen and Robert Torok in 2004.[2] The diagram in Figure 5.4 builds on the simple representation of ABC and includes the CAM-I activity-based budgeting loop. In line with the accepted interpretation of ABB, the CAM-I Closed Loop model suggests forecasting the level of demand (i.e. volume of sales), then working backwards to identify the amount of activity and resource requirements, ultimately leading to the line item expenses.

Effectively, the Closed Loop involves building an ABC model backwards. But rather than being a simple black box model, the CAM-I Closed Loop model incorporates some real-world decisions about comparing the amount of resource that is required with the amount of resource that is actually available or could be available within current capacity constraints so that "operational balance" is achieved. In essence, this means there is the correct amount of

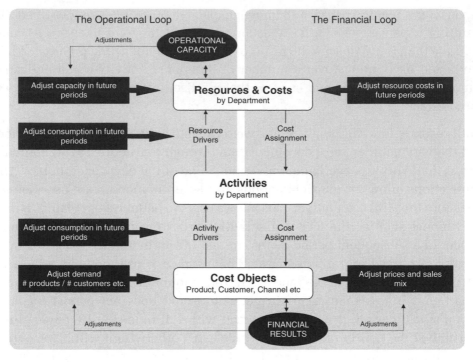

Figure 5.4 The CAM-I Closed Loop

resource to accommodate the new level of output without any access capacity. Once operational balance is achieved, attention is turned towards the financial balance; i.e. the cost of the resources required and the revenues. Here the organization can adjust the unit resource costs and the average selling prices of its products and services to achieve financial balance – the expectations or demands of the stakeholders. In essence, the CAM-I Closed Loop activity-based planning and costing model identifies five levers that can be adjusted to achieve balance:

Levers to achieve operational balance
- Sales volumes and sales mix
- Resource and activity consumption rates
- Resource capacity.

Levers to achieve financial balance
- Unit resource costs
- Unit prices for products and services.

Unlike traditional ABB models, the CAM-I Closed Loop model makes explicit the iterative nature of planning and budgeting, adjusting drivers (or levers as they call them), until the outcome is operationally feasible and financially optimal. It is a compelling model and seemingly little different to the concept of driver-based planning and budgeting proposed here. So where are the differences?

Differences between activity-based planning and budgeting and driver-based planning and budgeting

The authors of the Closed Loop model suggest that "While the Closed Loop model initially appears to be complex, there are only two necessary precursors; activity-based analysis and process analysis." The first is important in understanding the relationships between resources and activities; the second for understanding how sets of activities contribute to producing outputs such as products and services. Combining activity and process analyses gives activity-based information about activity and resource consumption rates and capacity constraints. Given that this type of detailed analysis across all cost centres and all line item expenses is a necessary prerequisite, it is not surprising to find the authors continuing: ". . . having an ABCM [activity-based cost management] process in place – and more importantly, having an activity-based mind set – will greatly simplify and assist in the implementation of ABPB [activity-based planning and budgeting]." Put bluntly, if you do not already have all this stuff at your fingertips, try to be positive about it, because it is going to be a major undertaking! Although it is not suggested that every line item expense should be included in an ABPB model, the requirement to do a detailed analysis of activities and processes is enough to deter all by the most committed from adopting ABB to replace their current budgeting process. This probably accounts for the scarcity of documented case studies of organizations that have adopted it; the book containing numerous worked examples but no real-world experiences. Activity-based budgeting is intellectually sound and probably represents best practice in planning and budgeting. It is just that in its pure form, it is too much for most organizations to digest.

However, it does have its place. Better functionality in recent software has overcome many of the limitations of simply back-calculating an ABC model, and now models can be iterative in the way the CAM-I Closed Loop model suggests with users adjusting levers to achieve operational and financial balance. This has led to a re-evaluation of the role of ABB and it is being increasingly adopted for long-range scenario planning by organizations that wish to underpin their strategic planning with a sound understanding of costs. WHSmith, one of the UK's leading retail groups, built a single model for both ABB and ABC and this is included in Appendix 3 as one of the few documented examples of an organization that routinely uses it.

Driver-based budgeting is certainly less onerous than ABB. Rather than being based on a detailed analysis of activities and processes, driver-based budgeting uses cause-and-effect relationships and the common-sense rules of thumb that managers already use to model their resource requirements and line item costs. As we have suggested, many of these same drivers will be used in an ABC model, but in driver-based budgeting there is no explicit activity layer and the use of drivers is based on experience rather than detailed analysis. In some departments such as a customer contact centre, many of the drivers such as average call duration and staff productivity will be accurately measured by call management systems. But other relationships used may be simple rule-of-thumb assumptions such as there should always be 5% overstaffing to allow for sickness and unanticipated absences. It might not be based on rigorous analysis; it might not be scientific, but it is what cost centre managers currently use and it is a good place to start. Run with these rule-of-thumb assumptions for a few periods and it will soon become apparent which are valid and which need further analysis and refinement.

By adopting this pragmatic and iterative approach, organizations can quickly implement driver-based budgeting with little need for detailed analysis. Start with the current understanding of the cost centre managers and work with the rules and assumptions they already use. Over a period of time, these can be refined and expanded until ultimately what started out as a driver-based budgeting model may be indistinguishable for an ABB model.

Unless their organization already has positive experience of ABC, anyone wishing to implement a predictive approach to planning and budgeting should perhaps stay clear of the "A" word. Mentioning activity-based anything is likely to frighten people off rather gain you sponsors and supporters. Many management accountants would perceive moving from traditional budgeting to a methodology such as driver-based budgeting to be complicated and something that may well meet with considerable resistance from budget contributors. We will come back to this misperception and how to best overcome it later when we get to discussing implementing driver-based budgeting.

Summary

If there is one message in this chapter, it is that driver-based planning and budgeting is a small idea that can bring big benefits. It is already happening inside most organizations and any finance department that wants to improve its budgeting process would be foolhardy to ignore it. Unlike ABB, there is no need for detailed activity analysis and organizations can develop a model starting with the rules, relationships and assumptions that cost centre managers already use today and gain immediate benefits. With experience, any model will gain sophistication and eventually there may be little discernable differences between a mature driver-based planning and budgeting model and an activity-based planning and budgeting model. But start with cost centre manager's everyday understanding of how demand drives resource requirements and expenses. It is far easier for most organizations to digest.

Notes

1 *Cost and Effect*, Kaplan, R.S. and Cooper, R., Harvard Business School Press 1998, ISBN 0–87584–788–9.
2 *The Closed Loop: Implementing Activity-Based Planning and Budgeting*, Stephen C. Hansen and Robert G. Torok (eds), CAM-I 2004, ISBN 1–59453–166–8.

The Pros and Cons of Driver-Based Budgeting

Benefits of driver-based budgeting

In Chapter 4, we documented a plethora of issues and challenges facing the traditional budgeting processes and detailed specific findings from a survey of companies showing that even those companies that had acquired packaged budgeting applications did not gain significant reductions in the time taken to prepare an annual budget or re-forecast nor did they re-forecast any more frequently. Having suggested that this is because these organizations have failed to address the end-to-end planning and budgeting process leaving cost centre managers still needing to do a considerable amount of off-line modelling on spreadsheets, driver-based budgeting has been proposed as a pragmatic alternative. However, before we start to document some of the benefits that organizations have gained when they have adopted driver-based budgeting, it should be pointed out that even driver-based budgeting has some limitations. It has considerable advantages over traditional budgeting, but it is still not the universal panacea, applicable in all types of industries and every department in any company. There are still pluses and minuses; but now the pluses outweigh the minuses by a considerable margin.

Driver-based planning and budgeting cuts the time to produce a budget or re-forecast

This is undoubtedly one of the major benefits and is one of the most attractive in that there are frequently tangible cost saving associated with driver-based budgeting. As a result of implementing a driver-based planning and budgeting process, Fortis Health, one of the case studies from Appendix 3, was able to complete a business-wide, bottom–up re-forecast involving every major department within three working days. Compared with the average of twelve reported in the survey referred to in Chapter 3, this represents a substantial improvement. What is perhaps more surprising is that the forecast looks forward a rolling 60 months, effectively bridging the gap between operational budgeting and strategic planning. The company was only able to do this because, having adopted driver-based planning and budgeting, individual cost centre managers were taking very little time every month to review and occasionally re-forecast non-financial drivers that generated a new set of line item expenses. Coupled with periodic strategic reviews, the company was effectively able to do away with the annual planning and budgeting cycle and simply send the appropriate calendar year forecast to their then parent company as their annual budget.

Driver-based planning and budgeting requires fewer iterations

Traditional budgets usually require a number of iterations before arriving at a compromise, which is both acceptable to senior management and tolerable to the cost centre managers who produced it. Invariably this is one of the reasons why the annual planning and budgeting cycle takes so long. In the past when senior management has demanded a reduction in expenses, cost centre managers have had to re-open their off-line spreadsheets and rework their planning assumptions to produce the reduction that has been requested. Doing this and then re-entering revised line item expenses into the enterprise planning and budgeting application takes time.

With a driver-based planning and budgeting model, iterations are undoubtedly faster. They will also be achieved with less disagreement as both sides have visibility of the underlying business drivers. They will be able to see both the historic trends and the forecasts for the coming year and be able to assess how best to achieve the desired reduction or even whether it is actually achievable without placing unreasonable demands on certain departments. If the driver-based planning and budgeting model has been built in a web-based application that can be recalculated by the user, this is typically an informed discussion that quickly reaches a resolution.

Driver-based planning and budgeting saves costs

Because the time to complete the annual budgeting cycle or produce a mid-year re-forecast is reduced and may require fewer iterations, there may be some cost savings. Most often this is in the finance department, where either the amount of overtime required during the annual budgeting cycle falls away, or one or more junior positions can be removed or redeployed to more beneficial tasks. There are also less obvious costs elsewhere. Many organizations come to a complete halt during the annual planning and budgeting cycle with managers locked away for days and sometimes weeks on end "doing the budget". In that their time could be more beneficially spent on managing the business shows, there is an opportunity cost here. It may not be a bankable cost-saving that will find its way to the bottom line, but freeing up management time for more value-adding activities brings benefits to the organization.

Driver-based budgets make managers accountable

There is no hiding with driver-based budgets. All the assumptions and off-line workings that are typically hidden away on disparate spreadsheets on managers' laptops are available for review. Whereas previously a departmental manager who had not exceeded their budgeted expenses might have escaped scrutiny, now they may find themselves in the spotlight as monthly reports show up declining productivity and pockets of excess capacity.

Because the logic built into many departmental driver-based budgets will start with some quantification of demand, such as the number of purchase orders to process or the number of sales leads to generate, it is a relatively simple step to calculate and report on some simple measures of unit cost. If the application selected for driver-based budgeting also provides functionality for ABC, these unit costs can be calculated very accurately including reassigned costs for IT and HR services provided by shared service units. Doing this can transform the entire debate around the monthly management report. It is no longer about whether the department is underspent or overspent. Now it is about what actions the departmental manager can take in future periods to keep the average unit cost on a steady downward trajectory. In a multi-site operation, these unit costs can be used in scorecards for comparative benchmarking, encouraging the type of intra-company competition and rivalry that leads to continual improvement.

Driver-based budgets help overcome the calendar year fixation

Many of the relationship and rules that are found in driver-based planning and budgeting models cross time periods. For instance, an event such as a sales order that occurs in one period creates demands, such as an invoice to issue and potentially an outstanding payment to chase that occur in other periods. Because of these cross period relationships, managers can see the impact that any actions they take have in future periods. So whereas previously they may have been tempted to take short-term actions such as cutting back on marketing activity towards the end of the year to ensure they hit their year-end targets and earn their bonus, now they might think twice. Starting a new financial year with a weak order book is not a good situation to be in, and the causality built into a driver-based planning and budgeting model will force managers to reflect before committing to decisions that they might live to regret.

Driver-based budgets provide insight and agility

A traditional monthly management report that shows actual expenditure against budgeted expenditure can make you happy or make you sad. But it cannot make you wiser. If the report shows a significant negative variance in a line item expense, someone is going to have to investigate the underlying root cause, assess what options are available to address the variance, agree with senior management what action is going to be taken and finally implement the chosen remedy. This is going to take some time and meanwhile the underlying root cause persists, adding unnecessary expense and dragging down financial performance. This is represented by the bottom line of the diagram in Figure 6.1.

In a driver-based budget, information about the underlying root cause behind the variance will be in the month-end report. It will, for instance, show that salary expenses are 20% above budgeted expenditure because the number of transactions processed during the period was above that originally forecasted and temporary staff had to be recruited at additional expense to cope. Knowing this, someone can quickly review the number of transactions forecast for future periods and quickly assess what actions to take; either hire some permanent staff

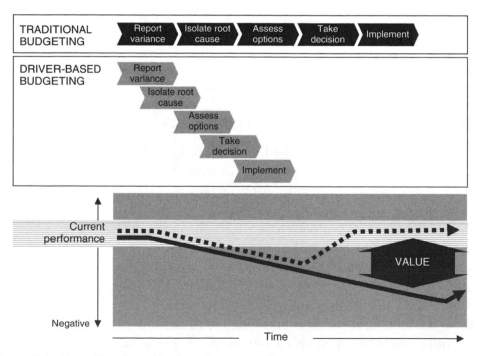

Figure 6.1 How driver-based budgets improve agility

or ride out the expense of temporary labour as the number of transactions is only a short-term phenomenon. The underlying root cause is isolated quickly; the impact of various options can be assessed in the budgeting model and the decision implemented sooner. This is represented by the dashed line in Figure 6.1. In our example the savings are small; no more than the difference in costs between full-time employees and temporary staff provided through an agency. In other situations, such as the early signs of an increase in customer attrition, the potential impact could be much larger. However, in both instances because the company is able to identify the underlying causality faster and be agile in implementing an appropriate remedy, it is creating value. In Figure 6.1, this is shown as difference between the two lines. Being able to quickly detect and assess the likely impact of the early signs of change in the internal and external environment is a capability worth having. It might enable you to get earnings back on track and save the organization from having to issue a profit warning that would have caused the share price to tumble. It might enable you to identify a growth opportunity and increase capacity quicker than your competitors.

Developing this deeper understanding of financial performance is essential to satisfying many of the recent requirements for forward-looking statements that are gradually finding their way into corporate reporting standards. Because driver-based budgeting integrates key non-financial drivers alongside traditional financial data in cause and effect relationships, it can help organizations develop a deeper understanding of their performance. When these forward-looking statements are formally included in the audit process, board members might take more interest in their planning and budgeting process; something that could stimulate the adoption of more dynamic methodologies such as driver-based budgeting.

But agility does not descend on organizations as if by magic. They need to work towards it, putting in place processes and systems that allow them to sense, assess and react quickly and decisively. Driver-based planning and budgeting is one of the fundamental building blocks for corporate agility – and may even be the keystone. Without it and the capability to thoroughly assess the impact that changes have on future profitability, quick responses to opportunities and threats are often little more than knee-jerk reactions.

Driver-based budgeting reduces risk

Driver-based budgeting allows the financial impact of different business scenarios to be rapidly assessed. Line item expenses, and ultimately bottom-line profitability, are the result of a mix of product and/or service volumes, operational drivers, productivity ratios and unit resource costs. In a driver-based planning and budgeting model, individual users can change any driver they have access to and immediately recalculate the model to show the impact on their responsibility centre. Similarly a senior manager or designated power user with access rights to the entire model can change any piece of information and recalculate the entire model to assess how overall profitability is affected. This means various scenarios can be developed and stored away to be called upon for a rainy day. But unlike many contingency plans, a driver-based scenario contains detailed information on how the organization needs to restructure itself to optimize profitability. Put yourself in the position of a chief executive of a poultry grower facing the uncertain impact of avian flu as it crept its way across mainland Europe. Could anyone predict whether consumers would stop eating chicken or not? And if they did, what actions needed to be taken in hatcheries and processing plants to take out capacity? With a driver-based planning and budget model in place, various scenarios could be developed and quickly deployed should consumer hysteria break out overnight. Having such detailed operating plans mitigates risk.

Driver-based budgets minimize extrapolation

Although certain line item expenses, such as facilities costs and audit fees, where there is no obvious driver, may still be increased by the simple extrapolation of prior period expenditure, this type of forecasting should be minimized in a driver-based budget. Certainly most of the controllable costs that are determined by sales and transaction volumes would be "driver-based".

Driver-based budgets are more accurate

Because driver-based budgets contain considerably less extrapolation so that expenses are more closely aligned with demand, they will be more accurate with less variance between forecasts and actual outcomes.

You can measure and track the accuracy of forecasts and reporting it back to cost centre managers will encourage them to be diligent in preparing their forecasts and will help to identify those who would benefit from some active involvement from the finance department. One way of doing this is to establish an appropriate measure of accuracy and have it automatically calculated as an ancillary line in month-end reports. Automating this with a simple rule in

Table 6.1   Monitoring the accuracy of expense forecasts

	April	May	June	July	August	September	October
Forecast done in March	£7,500	£7,400	£7,350	£7,375	£7,300	£7,250	£7,200
Forecast done in April		£7,350	£7,350	£7,300	£7,250	£7,000	£7,000
Forecast done in May			£7,300	£7,300	£7,200	£7,000	£6,900
Forecast done in June				£7,300	£7,150	£6,900	£6,800
Forecast done in July					£7,100	£6,800	£6,700
Forecast done in August						£6,800	£6,700
Forecast done in September							£6,800
							£6,750
Actual expenditure	£7,450	£7,400	£7,250	£7,350	£7,250	£6,550	£6,300
3-month accuracy			1.4%	0.3%	0.7%	5.8%	5.9%

software is quick and easy to achieve. For example, you might decide that a good measure of accuracy is a comparison of the last forecast done 3 months prior to each period with the actual expenditure for the period recorded after the event. Table 6.1 shows how this might work in an organization using rolling monthly re-forecasts with the shaded cells indicating which figures are being compared to calculate the measure of accuracy.

In this example, the cost centre manager has produced fairly accurate forecasts of expenditure until the two most recent months and this may be a signal that they need outside assistance. Clearly, it is impractical to monitor the accuracy of every line item and having single measure for each cost centre total is probably sufficient both to motivate users to improved accuracy and to highlight those who need help.

Driver-based budgets drive out excess capacity

One of the benefits of systematically modelling resource requirements and comparing them against the amount of resource actually provided is that excess capacity is automatically calculated and made visible across the organization. Many disparate operational systems might contain some measures of capacity utilization, but in a driver-based budget, these can all be brought together and reported in one place with an associated cost put against it. The most obvious areas of a business to do this are those with highly repetitious activities and a large amount of controllable costs, particularly staff costs.

Even when using the most sophisticated techniques, forecasts are never going to be consistently accurate. The challenge is to continually re-forecast and align resources with changes in demand. This is an intrinsic part of any driver-based budgeting model. General insurance is a sector with a particular requirement for capacity planning models. When premium rates are high, insurers increase their capacity and write more new business. Inevitability this leads to over-capacity in the market and competitive forces cause premiums to soften. At this point, many insurers turn their focus from premium growth to margin management and pull back in certain areas of business, waiting until there is a market-wide adjustment in premiums before entering expansion mode once more. Managing this cycle calls for sensitive forward-looking systems for modelling demand and capacity and driver-based budgeting can provide this.

Driver-based budgets enable organizations to forecast more frequently

Many drivers used in driver-based budgets are the type of metrics that managers work with on a regular basis. In certain situations, such as customer contact centres, they will be reviewing them and managing them in real time. In most situations, the driver will be a metric that is reported on a weekly or monthly basis, such things as the number of new sales orders, the rate of customer attrition or the average selling price of products and services. Some of information about these drivers will be almost instantaneously available from core operational systems. This means cost centre managers can easily and quickly review and update drivers, effectively re-forecasting the entire budget with no more than a handful of key business drivers. Because this involves so little time and effort, organizations can afford to re-forecast more frequently without taking managers away from their day-to-day responsibilities and without the risk of generating resistance from the contributors. Without moving towards a dynamic, driver-based planning and budgeting process, it is doubtful whether many organizations could achieve the frequency of forecasting they aspire to. It is a prerequisite of monthly rolling re-forecasting.

In a traditional budgeting process, making changes to a budget would either take multiple iterations backwards and forwards to the individual cost centre managers or would require someone simply making top–down amendments to line item expenses without a full understanding of how the changes they are making might restrict the organization's ability to satisfy the anticipated level of demand. Such exercises in breaking back a reduction in expenses across lower level responsibility centres are the antithesis of driver-based budgeting.

Driver-based budgeting minimizes "gaming"

As discussed in Chapter 4, cost centre managers who have some element of bonus payment tied into the budget tend to game especially if they know there is a little chance of being caught out. The game is to secure a greater budget allocation that is actually required and a smaller revenue target than what can comfortably be achieved. A skilled negotiator can have their bonus in the bag almost before the new financial year has begun. With driver-based budgets, causal relationships are transparent and this can limit the opportunity for gaming. There is simply less opportunity to hoodwink senior management if all the workings and assumptions are laid out for everyone to see.

Some of the drivers that are fundamental to a driver-based budget may also be key metrics in any scorecards used inside the organization. Where negotiated performance targets have been abandoned and the organization has moved towards rewarding people on relative measures such as improvements over previous periods, they will find undoubted value in a driver-based budget. The metrics against which managers are rewarded are likely to be part of their individual or departmental scorecard. But a scorecard will only report and trend these metrics. What managers need is a tool to test out new initiatives that will help them to deliver continual improvements. This is a role a driver-based budget fulfils.

Downsides of driver-based budgeting

This exhaustive list of the benefits that can be gained from moving towards driver-based planning and budgeting might suggest that it is the universal panacea to every organization's pain points with their budgeting process. This is not the case. Driver-based planning and budgeting has its shortcomings and it is only fair to identify them so that they can be thought about and accommodated into implementation plans.

Driver-based budgeting is perceived to be difficult to implement

Even though it requires considerably less time and effort than ABB, driver-based budgeting is perceived to be difficult to implement. Even open-mined accountants who are actively seeking better ways to budget and attend seminars on driver-based planning and budgeting put this at the top of their list of reservations.

One can speculate on the reasons that underpin this misperception. As was discussed in Chapter 5, many writers have developed increasingly sophisticated methodologies that have evolved out of ABC. While many budget controllers may have encountered this subject earlier in their career, at some point they have taken the decision to move away from cost accounting and develop their career in other directions. Suggesting they should now abandon their current budgeting process and implement something based on activities or even drivers is likely to be alien to them. What people need is an easy first step rather than an overwhelming methodology.

There are two approaches to negating this objection:

1. Many cost centres managers inside most organizations are already doing driver-based planning and budgeting and the finance function would benefit from having better visibility of what these people are doing. Most management accountants will agree that they all have a handful of cost centre managers who support their budget submissions with "working papers" in the form of spreadsheets with rules. All we are talking about is incorporating these into the budgeting system.
2. Many management accountants have never built a driver-based budget and benefit from working through an exercise such as the one included in Appendix 1 using a spreadsheet package. The hands-on experience of translating the business logic into a set of rules and writing some simple formulas soon removes any apprehension and most become enthusiastic converts.

Having gone through such an exercise, most people will have a sound understanding of what is involved in building a driver-based planning and budgeting model. They will be pleasantly surprised at how little time and effort is involved and have experienced at first hand how easy and quick it is to re-forecast the model. For many, it is a defining moment; they understand what it is all about and how it is a simple progression from what is already happening in some parts of their organization. We will come back to using this type of experiential learning when we discuss implementation issues.

"Cost centre managers don't know the rules"

It is not unusual for management accountants to claim that their "cost centre managers don't know the rules". While there may be some cost centre managers who are new to their department and have yet to go through the planning involved in compiling a budget submission, I have yet to meet an experienced manager who does not understand what drives expenses in their department. Even those managers that have traditionally added an incremental increase to last year's line item expenses to generate next year's budget submission can fluently discuss how changes in demand impacts resource requirements and costs. It is a small step for them to convert their understanding and assumptions into rules and relationships and translate them into formulas.

Driver-based budgets are difficult to maintain

It is not good practice to hard code any number used by a rule in a driver-based planning and budgeting model. Some day you will come to regret it. For instance, the line item expense for pensions may have been $7\frac{1}{2}$% of salary costs for as along as anyone can remember and there may be a temptation to hard code the number into a formula used across all departments, periods and versions of your model. It might not fluctuate every period like the cost of a litre of fuel, but one day the company pension policy might be renegotiated, so leave all the drivers as variables that can be changed every period. It is easier in the long run.

But otherwise driver-based budgets are no more difficult to maintain than any other budget. The structure of the model will need to be amended to accommodate new departments, new reporting structures and new products and in most packaged budgeting applications this is easy to do. But the rules and relationships that underpin a driver-based planning and budgeting model are fairly static. The number of claims that need to be assessed will always be a factor of the number of live policies and the claims frequency. The number of live policies and the claims frequency will fluctuate, but the rule itself will hold for all periods and version in the model and requires zero maintenance.

In a rolling model, rules need to be written differently to account for the fact that the model includes actual revenues and expenses up to the current period and forecast revenues and expenses in future periods. For instance, if we are looking at actual expenses, the average monthly salary costs of staff is calculated by dividing the salary expenses (a figure imported from the general ledger), by the number of staff (a figure that may be imported from the HR system). But if we are looking at forecast expenses, the number of staff and the average monthly staff cost are figures that are multiplied to calculate the line item expenses for salaries. If you wanted to write such a rule in a spreadsheet, you would need to flag each month as being either "Year to Date" (YTD) or "Year to Go" (YTG) and write an "IF, THEN" function. The calculation logic would vary depending on whether the month was part of YTD or YTG and every time the model was replenished with new data, the flag for the corresponding month would need to be changed. Achieving this in a packaged budgeting application is just as straightforward using attributes for flagging each period as YTD or YTG.

A driver based planning and budgeting model incorporates more data that a traditional budget that includes only line item expenses and this can suggest there is an onerous amount of maintenance involved in maintaining a model. This is not the case.

- Relatively few line item expenses will be calculated by drivers and rules. In most driver-based planning and budgeting models, it is only those line items such as salaries and other controllable costs that are calculated using drivers and rules. Most line item expenses remain as simple data entry lines just as in a traditional budget.
- Most models rely on a limited number of drivers. In many departments, there is likely to be no more than a forecast of demand, a consumption ratio, a resource requirement and unit cost of resource. Some of the additional non-financial line items will be calculated from other data held in the model and much of the data, such as staff numbers and staff productivity, will already be held in other recording and processing systems across the organization. In many instances, the amount of data required to populate a model is so small that it is not worthwhile automating monthly data imports. For example, the key drivers for planning and budgeting staff resources in a customer contact centre are the number of calls, the productivity of staff and the unit cost of staff – three additional pieces of data that can be manually updated from other systems.
- Today much of this information is being maintained on spreadsheets on individual managers' desktops. This is inefficient. It is also invisible to the rest of the organization and cannot be utilized by anyone other than to the cost centre manager who maintains it and uses it to model their resource requirements and line item expenses. It has to be better to maintain it in one system so that it can be maintained and, if necessary, validated under the control by finance function and made available to the entire enterprise.

Driver-based budgeting needs managing as a process

With traditional budgeting, it is all too easy for finance to prepare the input sheets, issue them manually or electronically to the cost centre managers and sit back and wait until the completed budget submissions are received. If one department has to wait upon the output of another before they can start their planning and budgeting, it is something for them to sort out between themselves without finance being involved. With driver-based budgeting where the output of one department becomes the input of another, it is much more important to identify and manage the sequence in which various departments prepare and submit budgets and re-forecasts. This now becomes the explicit responsibility of finance.

Working with departmental managers will soon determine the flow of information and identify the necessary sequence. In smaller organizations with a limited number of cost centre managers, the process can be managed by establishing a timetable and using e-mail and telephone reminders to keep everyone on track. In larger organizations with potentially hundreds of budget contributors, managing the process is likely to require a workflow tool, something that is integral to most packaged budgeting applications. These tools allow an administrator to map the required budget or re-forecast submission and authorization process and automate all the necessary e-mail alerts and reminders. Cost centre managers automatically receive an e-mail to tell them they can start work on their budget, together with a hyperlink to the appropriate input page if a web-based planning and budgeting package is being used. Should the submission not have been received as the deadline approaches, further e-mails can be triggered to both the cost centre manager and their superior. If the deadline has lapsed and still nothing has been received, the previous submission can be automatically rolled forward. A similar process can be developed for senior managers to review and authorize submissions, automatically routing rejected submissions back to departmental managers for reworking.

This type of tool allows budget administrators to expedite both the annual planning and the budgeting process and mid-year re-forecasts, saving away routines to call upon month after month. Using them in conjunction with a driver-based budget has enabled organizations to slash the time it takes to budget and re-forecast, in one instance completing a tightly sequenced, enterprise-wide re-forecast involving over a hundred contributors in three working days. A quick review and update, then onto the next person down the line in quick succession.

Driver-based budgets can be perceived to be deterministic

Because driver-based planning and budgeting models use rules and relationships to predict certain resource requirements and line item expenses, cost centre managers may perceive them as being "deterministic" and eroding their authority and control. If this issue goes unaddressed it can fester and become a source of resistance during the implementation process.

In reality, there is always going to be a variance between the amounts of resource a driver-based planning and budgeting model predicts is required and what is actually provided. For example, a model may predict that two additional time equivalents are required in 2 months' time. However, due to problems in recruiting skilled staff, these positions are not recruited in time and the increased workload has to be accommodated using overtime and temporary staff. The departmental manager made informed decisions along the way and the eventual outcome was a difference in resources and possibly cost between what the model predicted and what was actually provided. Everyone accepts that not everything turns out exactly as predicted; that's why we have managers.

Similarly a departmental manager should be under no obligation to provide the exact amount of resource that a model predicts. They may wish to overstaff by a few percentage points to allow for unplanned absences, training and holidays, and a rule could be built into the model to incorporate this. They may wish to overstaff because they have a small team of people who have been taken away from their day-to-day tasks and given a special project to work on. If this is a one-off or infrequent event, it is hardly worth building rules in to a model to reflect it. Most packaged budgeting applications allow users to add a commentary against any item of data, and in such instances the manager could simply add a note to let others know that his departmental headcount will be out of kilter for a couple of months.

One way to convey the message that the driver-based budget is not a top–down deterministic tool that departmental managers must abide to at every turn is to put breaks into the logic. Doing this allows managers to override a number generated by rules in the model with a figure of their own. It does not make sense to allow managers to override the logic in every rule. For instance, there is no reason why you would ever allow a mail room manager to override a calculated expense for postage. But breaking the logic in some parts of a model is a desirable feature and does get across the message that the individual manager is still in control. Staff planning is a prime example. A driver-based model may include line items to show the predicted number of hours of resource and predicted number of FTEs that are required during a specific period. But underneath this can be left an empty row where the manager can enter an override number, which, if present, would be referenced to calculate departmental salary costs and other expenses. It is a simple point, but it overcomes potential resistance and leaves manager's feeling in control.

Some line items, departments and businesses do not lend themselves to driver-based budgeting

Much as I and other writers support driver-based, dynamic or predictive planning and budgeting, it cannot be used in every situation. In fact you may have enthusiastically read this book this far only to be disappointed by the next few lines. If that is the case, I apologise. Give or better still, sell, the book to someone who is better able to make use of the methodology and encourage them to adopt it. That way, at least you will get some second-hand experience that may help you in some future role. But for the moment, let us be blunt:

- Every department is likely to have some line item expenses such as subscriptions and professional fees that are hardly driver-based and may just as well be entered as if in a traditional budget.
- Certain departments such as legal, internal audit, marketing and the chief executive's office do not perform highly repetitive activities and most of their line item expenses may not lend themselves to driver-based planning and budgeting. Work with them to identify how they currently plan and budget, but be prepared to let them budget in the same way they always have.
- Some businesses and organizations may not lend themselves to driver-based planning and budgeting. This has nothing to do with whether they are commercial businesses, public sector or not-for-profit organizations. It all depends on what they do. For instance, in many ways a direct insurer and a government agency processing passport applications may not appear to have much in common. However, they both carry out highly standardized and repetitive activities that lend themselves to driver-based budgeting. Change the level of demand and the whole resource plan needs updating. On the other hand, there is less opportunity to deploy driver-based planning and budgeting in an advertising agency and or a fire department where there always needs to be a predetermined level of resource constantly ready to attend to any emergency. But even in these organizations you will always find some line item expenses, such as pensions, which are rule-driven. There just will not be as much scope for deploying driver-based budgeting as there is in other industries.

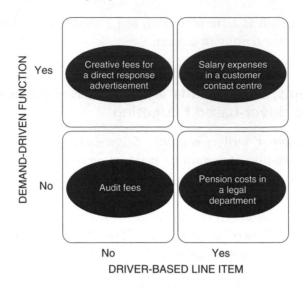

Figure 6.2 Matrix of driver-based functions and driver-based line items

The grid shown in Figure 6.2 below may help you identify which departments and which line items are "driver-based" in your organization. This is a useful tool for working with line managers once they have grasped the core idea behind driver-based budgeting. Shown a couple of examples, they will quickly decide which half of the matrix their department falls into and identify exactly which line items lend themselves to driver-based budgeting and which do not. Use it either to select which department to work with in producing a pilot study, or more generally to help line managers begin to formulate their own departmental model.

Some people may be uncomfortable with the transparency that comes with driver-based budgeting

As we have mentioned previously, driver-based planning and budgeting minimizes the opportunity for managers to game and makes ·people more accountable for the resources under their control. While the majority are likely to quickly assimilate the new transparency and focus on driving the business forward, there may be one or more managers who, for whatever reason, resent the ability of their immediate superiors to scrutinize the logic and assumptions in their budget submissions. If you are seen as the internal champion of the new method of planning and budgeting, you may well be the target of their dissent. However, you are not their manager and it may be unwise to try and personally address their grievances. It is better to use accepted reporting lines, inform their manager and let them resolve the situation.

Summary

Driver-based planning and budgeting addresses many of the shortcomings of traditional budgeting. It makes budgeting and re-forecasting quicker (and therefore less costly) and enables organizations to re-forecast much more frequently providing better visibility into the future. But because driver-based planning and budgeting is based on a dynamic model of the organization that incorporates both internal and external non-financial drivers and dynamically links revenue of expenses, it also brings other benefits. It helps align resources across the enterprise, eliminating pockets of excess capacity and it can be used as a simulation engine that managers can use to test out scenarios before committing to action. All this helps organizations to sense, assess and respond to external and internal changes quicker, giving them the agility they seek and the decisiveness to act in a concerted manner.

Despite these compelling benefits, driver-based budgeting is not for everyone. It is most applicable to certain, but by no means all, line item expenses in departments with a high volume of highly repetitious activities and a high proportion of controllable or variable costs. Because of this it is best suited to "driver-based" industries such as insurance, logistics and certain high-volume government services such as those processing passport applications and patent applications. But even here, it has to be accepted that some line item expenses are simply not driver based. The key thing is those that are driver based are critical to organization's financial performance.

Budgeting for Shared Services

So far we have proposed moving to driver-based planning and budgeting for those line item expenses that are driven by demand and that this will help organizations overcome many of the shortcomings of traditional budgeting enabling them to re-forecast more frequently and keep resources aligned with fluctuating revenues. At the same time, it has also been suggested that the methodology is not for all line item expenses and all departments and is more applicable to some industries than others. For the most part, the examples that have been developed are from front-line operations, and what has not been mentioned is the support functions that every organization has in some shape or form; the main ones being IT, HR and Finance. To keep things simple, we will call these "shared services", although that in no way implies that they are necessarily located apart from operational units or even located offshore in some distant country. The objective of this chapter is simply to explore how driver-based planning and budgeting applies to the support functions wherever they may be. Because IT is typically the most costly of the support functions, we will use it as the focus for our discussion, but the principles that will be developed apply to any other support function.

In sectors such as telecommunications and financial services, the IT function alone can account for a quarter of total costs. Yet in many instances there is a limited understanding of what is driving the resources and costs tied up in IT. When CEO's sought cost-savings in the past, they typically looked to the direct costs in the business. But these have been shaved back to the bone and now CEO's must seek to understand the costs they have tied up in IT and other corporate shared service functions, as these are becoming the only remaining opportunity for significant cost savings.

Many large organizations have introduced shared services business units in order to realize economies of scale, and therefore reduce the total cost of corporate support functions. While this may result in a step change in total IT costs, other challenges remain. With all IT support centralized, how do you ensure that IT is accountable to the business units it supports and that its resources are aligned with the needs of the business units? Having proposed a transparent approach to resource planning within operating units, how do we ensure that an equally rigorous approach is used for calculating cross-charges for shared services back to the business units? How can you justify these costs and keep them aligned with demand? Having developed a more disciplined approach to planning and budgeting for the front-line operations, the shared services functions cannot be ignored. If they were ever allowed to carry on

Co-operative Insurance Services (CIS)

Formed in 1867, Co-operative Insurance Services (CIS) is the only co-operative in the UK insurance sector, with 4.5 million customers and more than £20 billion of funds under its management. Its parent, the Co-operative Group, is one of the world's largest consumer co-operatives, owned and controlled by its members, serving millions of people across the UK with a diverse product offering including food retailing, holidays, banking, insurance, cookware and funeral services.

As the insurance market has become more competitive following successive mergers and new entrants, CIS recognized the need to develop a better understanding of how individual products were incurring costs. To provide reliable costing information in a complex multi-product and multi-channel business, it was also recognized that traditional costing techniques would be insufficient. Fortunately, CIS had already deployed ABC, and knew that it could provide a robust methodology for allocating expenses when costing products. CIS use the ABC data to accurately assign IT costs to the departments and products that consume IT activities. The IT department itself carries no residual cost as all costs are continually allocated out of IT into other departments.

Information Technology provides seven principal services under the following headings:
1. New Systems
2. Desktop Support
3. Mid-range System Support
4. Mainframe System Support
5. Communication Services (e-mail)
6. Laptop Services
7. Data Preparation.

Information Technology personnel enter their activities on timesheets and mark them against the various codes in their database. Each of the codes represents an activity against one of the services listed, categorized by product or product group. So, for example, when a manager requests IT support to run a data extract, the cost of performing that activity is allocated out of IT into his cost centre. According to CIS, having an existing timesheet system in place and an IT Manager with a strong customer focus were the key success factors for implementing shared services costing.

budgeting in the same way that they always did, whatever that was, front line business managers would rightly be asking questions.

In many organizations, cross-charges are a constant source of irritation and bickering between the shared services provider and the business units. This is because there is often a limited understanding of how the demands of the business unit influence these costs and because cross-charges are often little more than a simple apportionment of total IT costs. To develop a deeper understanding of how and why IT costs are incurred and provide a firm basis for cross-charging, many shared services units are using ABC, something that has been expanded on in Appendix 2. Not only does this provide detailed information to business units about their consumption of central resources, it also provides a common understanding for making informed decision to reduce shared services costs.

After several years of cost reduction in many sectors, business units that carry the majority of direct costs are likely to have little left to cut without impairing their ability to carry out their main activities. The pie chart in Figure 7.1 shows expenses taken from a cost centre of a telecommunications provider. Here over half the costs carried by the responsibility manager's profit and loss account are allocations from shared services departments or other corporate overheads. Should this enterprise be seeking a further 3% reduction in costs, essentially this manager only has two options: to try to remove 6% from his own direct

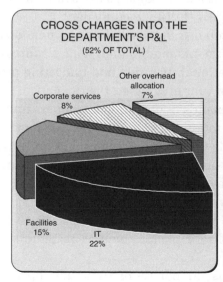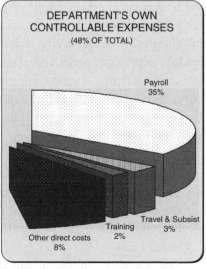

Figure 7.1 Example of a cost centre's expenses in the telecommunications sector

costs, most of which are to do with people; or to lobby the executive to critically examine the costs of the shared services functions. In such a situation, anyone who had introduced driver-based planning and budgeting to the rest of the operation and not the support functions would be putting their head on the chopping block!

In recent years, many organizations have effectively reduced the costs of providing support services to simply by concentrating them in corporate shared services units. This resulted in a step change in the costs of support services such as IT, HR and Facilities and was considered to be "best practice". With the phenomenal growth of outsourcing, there are opportunities to cut the costs of shared services functions even further, moving them to local third party providers or even across continents where the required skills can be sourced for a fraction of local costs. Again this will result in a step change in the cost of support services and may give an enterprise a temporary cost advantage over its competitors.

However, despite the gains to be had by building shared services departments and by locating them where the required skills can be obtained at the lowest cost, many organizations still have a limited understanding of the dynamics of the shared services functions. In essence, there are two related issues:

1. *Understanding the cost of shared services.* Despite being a large proportion of an enterprise's costs, in many organizations the costs of shared services functions such as IT and HR are simply apportioned to the profit and loss accounts of business units based on some easily available metric, such as revenue, headcount or FTEs (full-time equivalents).

2. *Aligning the resources in shared services units with business unit forecasts of demand.* Shared service departments tend to plan their resources and budget separately from the operational planning and budgeting process of business units. As the financial year progresses, the capacity of shared services departments and the demands of operational business units can become grossly misaligned. The following scenario is not uncommon
   - The business units produce their operational plans and budgets.
   - The shared services units construct their own operational plans and budgets with a cursory glance at those of the business units.
   - The butgets of the shared services functions are approved and apportioned to the business units' profit and loss accounts for the coming year, based on some arbitrary metric, such as revenue split or headcount.
   - The majority of organizations do not re-forecast their operational plans or budgets as frequently as they wish, so that inevitably the

demands of the business units and the capacity of the shared services functions can easily become misaligned.

- As the year progresses, any variance above the budgeted cost of the shared services functions that appears on a responsibility centre manager's monthly management reports becomes an increasing source of frustration and annoyance. The shared services provider cannot adequately explain it; the responsibility centre manager, who has been ruthlessly managing his own direct costs throughout the year, can only argue that the apportionment is unfair and that other business units should pick up more. Neither the shared services provider nor the responsibility centre manager has sufficient insight to have a productive discussion. The result is anguish and frustration.

At the same time, the boards and executives of many organizations grapple with authorizing continuing investment from shared services functions such as IT without insight as to how such expenditure relates to the demands of the business units or how it will impact long-term profitability. Regardless of whether shared services are provided in-house or by a third party, organizations need far better insight into these costs and particularly the costs of the IT function, which for many is simply a black hole.

To fully understand the costs of the IT function so they can be allocated to the business units in line with the way in which they consume IT resources, any costing and cross-charging methodology needs to:

- Correctly allocate IT costs from the general ledger to the services that IT provides to the business units.
- Capture and incorporate other costs from other departments that should be allocated to the provision of IT services. These may include such things as property costs from the Facilities cost centre, and recruitment and payroll costs from the HR cost centre.
- Realistically reflect that just as HR provides services to IT, IT provides services to HR – and that to calculate the true cost of providing a service, these reciprocal costs should be passed between these departments reiteratively until they become insignificant, whilst still providing an audit trail.
- Capture and reflect the fact that different business units use IT services in different ways. For instance, some business units may have a need for secure payment processing over the web in addition to more general firewall and anti-viral security on the desktop network.

- Capture and reflect the fact that certain parts of the business may use the same service differently. For example, an IT service such as Help Desk support may be allocated to business units based on the number of times they use it. However, due to a lack of internal expertise, the time taken to resolve the Help Desk queries for some business units may be far in excess of others.

Given the complexity that can result from multiple line items, services, cost drivers and business units, as well as the need for being able to trace cross-charges right back through the allocations to line items in the general ledger, the only way to reliably understand complex shared services costs is by adopting an ABC methodology and deploying an application capable of managing the true multidimensionality of the costs involved.

How ABC might apply to IT shared services costing

While some line item costs that appear in the general ledger of an IT department might be relatively easy to understand and can be directly allocated to a business unit, many line item costs will need to be re-allocated to new cost pools, where they can be combined with other costs from the departments that provide support to IT, such as HR and Facilities. Some of these cost pools may then be allocated directly to services, but the majority will be allocated to the activities that IT staff perform to better understand how they relate to the services the IT function provides. Figure 7.2 shows how ABC might be applied to costing IT shared services. Note that not all costs need be taken through the activity layer. Certain IT costs, such as the cost of hardware and software for a customer relationship management (CRM) system that is only used by one division can be assigned directly to that division. However, the other expenses associated with providing this system such as network costs and IT salary expenses that are "shared" with other internal customers will need taking through an activity layer so they can be correctly assigned.

Evidently, the cost of hardware and software need to be amortized over their lifetime to avoid spikes in calculated costs at the time of the investment. Much of this data can be directly imported into the ABC model from the asset register. Similarly many IT departments deploy time capture systems to record the amount of time staff such as programmers spent on individual projects and data from these systems can be directly imported saving considerable effort in collecting non-system driver data.

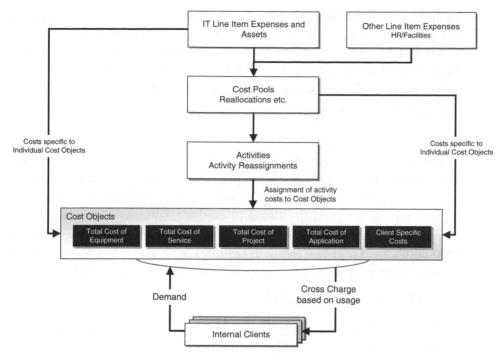

Figure 7.2 Example of the flow of costs in a IT shared services costing model

Standardized service definitions

Organizations frequently benchmark their IT costs against their industry peers and this has led to companies that have adopted ABC to adopt one of the standardized service definitions as cost objects. The IT Infrastructure Library (ITIL), which was created by the UK Government, is rapidly being adopted across the world as the standard for best practice in the provision of IT Service. However there are others in use.

Options for cross-charging

Once the total cost of a service is calculated, there are various options for calculating a unit rate for cross-charging the business units for their use of the service:

- **Demand-based pricing**

  If the organization wishes to fully allocate the total cost of the IT function across the business units, the unit rate charge is typically based on the total cost of the service during the period, divided by the actual demand for the service during the period. This leaves the IT function with no residual costs. This can be represented by the equation below where $TC(x)^t$ is the total cost of service (x) during period t, $TD(x)^t$ is the total demand for the service during period t, and $UPD(x)^t$ is the unit price of the service based on demand for the service during the period

$$TC(x)^t/TD(x)^t = UPD(x)^t$$

- **Capacity-based pricing**
  However, other options are possible. The rate could be based on the total cost of the service during the period, divided by the amount of the service available during the period; that is, based on the capacity of the IT function rather than the demand of the business units. Here, if the service is over-resourced and IT is able to provide more than the business units consume, IT will be left with residual costs and this may drive them to reduce capacity during the next period. The formula now becomes:

$$TC(x)^t/TCap(x)^t = UPCap(x)^t$$

However some shared services units are operating as profit centres and in these instances, ABC may be used to calculate a rate based on either of the methodologies above, to which a fixed or percentage mark-up may be added before being charged out to the business units.

Ultimately the choice of pricing methodology can lead to an under- or over-recovery of IT costs. Unless rules are set for how any under- or over-recovery of IT costs will be balanced out in future periods, this give rise to resentment from the business units that they are "over-charged". Organizations should also explore whether it is prudent to have under- or over-recovered amounts in their year-end accounts and may wish to involve their auditors in this discussion.

Benefits of using ABC in IT shared services costing and cross-charging

Having adopted an ABC methodology for costing IT services, the organization will have a detailed understanding of the services provided by IT, the activities involved in providing them and how they consume resources and costs. Detailed invoices can be produced showing the business units' use of the service, the unit price and the total cross-charge, and should more detail be required, with an ABC methodology, the costs can be traced back to their origin.

But by fully understanding what activities are consuming resources and costs, and which are value-adding or non-value-adding, the business unit and the IT function are better placed to enter into a dialogue and understand how they can work together to reduce costs. This may involve no more than taking simple steps to adjust service levels such as response times or batching transaction processing to give reduced set up costs. It has been reported that removing non-value-adding activities can help to reduce costs by as much as 5%. This is far in excess of the cost of deploying ABC, giving an immediate return on any investment.

Aligning shared services resource with the business needs

A second challenge for organizations is to frequently realign the resource and capacity of shared services functions with the needs of the business units. For this to happen, organizations need to progress towards more frequent re-forecasting so that business units are routinely updating the key non-financial data that drives their shared services demands. The shared services functions can then use this information to realign their own resource requirements for the coming periods, taking their actual costs through an ABC methodology to calculate monthly cross-charges that are passed back to the business units. Let us develop some examples.

Suppose everyone in a large department in a business unit needs a personal computer and that headcount in this department fluctuates with sales volumes or some other measure of demand. Then the number of PCs required each period should be included as a line item in the departmental budget, and the consolidated number for the organization's total requirement should be made available to the IT department. That way they can schedule their purchases, and plan and cost the resources they need to commission new PCs, decommission and replace old PCs and staff the helpdesk facility. Many other services that IT provides can be budgeting for in exactly the same way. There are a number of benefits of adopting this driver-based approach to planning and budgeting in shared services units.

- Because the IT resource plan and budget has been built from information that the business units have provided, it should be more accurate as should the forecast for the cross-charge that the business units will receive during the financial year.

- Each time the business units re-forecast during the year, IT receives a new forecast of demand for each of its services and can realign its own resources to accommodate any changes. Many of the resources in IT, such as support staff and even data storage, can be predicted using driver-based rules and many even have capacity constraints which need to be identified well into the future. These can be programmed into a driver-based model with automated alerts to direct management attention to impending bottlenecks.
- Every month, the business unit can be sent an invoice detailing the amount of each service it consumed, the unit price the service is being provided at and the total amount being cross-charged. This can even be compared with the figures in the original budget and a full variance analysis provided. Doing this provides the business unit with complete insight into its cross-charge and what is actually driving it. There should be fewer surprises and much less argument. And if the business unit wishes to reduce its cross-charge, it has sufficient information to have an informed discussion with IT and decide how best this could be achieved. It might be by accepting a lower service standard and abandoning its traditional daily printing run. Equally it might be by gradually downgrading the specification of some desktop computers.

That was an example of using drivers in certain line item expenses in IT budgets. Exactly the same principle applies to certain line items in HR and Finance:

- Staffing requirements in future periods can be compared with current establishment to calculate the number of new recruits needed in each future period and this figure used to driver staffing requirements and even recruitment advertising costs in a busy HR department.
- The anticipated number of purchase orders and invoices generated by internal customers can be used for resource planning and budgeting staff costs in a large finance shared services unit.

Shared services and support functions that handle large volumes of repetitious activities such as recruitment and fleet administration are little different to any other front-line operational unit. Certain line items in any shared services budget lend themselves to driver-based planning and budgeting and including the support functions in an enterprise-wide implementation will provide some glue that helps keep them aligned with changing business needs. The business units will certainly thank you for including them in the initiative. And given the pressure that many chief information officers and their colleagues who head up the other support functions are under to become more accountable, they are likely to demonstrate their support.

Groupe Casino

With over 7000 stores throughout France trading under 40 fascias, including Géant, Casino Supermarché, Monoprix, Casino Superstores and Casino Supermarkets, Groupe Casino has gained a leading edge in the French food retail trade and has an enviable financial performance with an improvement in earnings per share in each of the last 5 years.

In order to streamline its IT costs, Groupe Casino created a dedicated division, Casino Information Technology (IT), to co-ordinate all of its computer assets under one roof. Organized into departments (Analysis, Production, Technical, Financial, etc.), Casino IT provides all subsidiaries of Groupe Casino with their IT services. Previously, Casino IT used a complex system based on data collected from various spreadsheets for costing and cross-charging. This proved difficult to use for controlling the company's activities and communicating across the entire organization. Concerned with transparency and wishing to establish optimal cost management, Casino IT implemented an ABC application that would enable it to:

- Receive input automatically from existing systems used to measure the amount of processing time or storage capacity business units consumed and track the time IT staff and developers spent on tasks for different businesses.
- Calculate the costs of services provided.
- Automatically cross-charge these to its forty internal customers based on their use of the services with a fully detailed invoice of how these charges were calculated.

The solution that Casino IT implemented helped them achieve their goals by ensuring each and every department, branch or subsidiary in Groupe Casino is billed with the highest degree of accuracy for the IT services they use. Casino IT has also ensured that each business is responsible for their consumption of IT services and has better control over the volumes of services and hardware they purchase. It will also provide Casino IT managers with a tool for controlling costs of the projects they personally manage.

Summary

Implementing a driver-based planning and budgeting across an organization without involving the shared services functions is likely to cause resentment particularly from managers in those cost centres and business units that receive a high proportion of cross-charges. If there is an initiative to improve the frequency of re-forecasting, agility and ultimately accountability in the business units, the shared services units should always be included. Shared services units face two challenges: improving the accuracy and transparency of their costing, and improving their planning and budgeting. Figure 7.3 can be used to represent where an organization's shared services functions might lie in terms of their costing and planning.

The vertical axis represents the accuracy and transparency of their shared services costing and cross-charging, while the horizontal axis represents the degree to which the planning and budgeting of the business units and the shared services provider are aligned and integrated. As such, the top left quadrant represents any organization that has already adopted an ABC methodology for costing IT shared services and is highly accountable to the business units. But having implemented a reliable and robust costing methodology, their challenge is now to receive more frequent forecasts of demand from the internal business users so that they can keep their own resources and operational costs

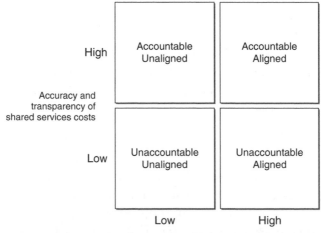

Figure 7.3   Shared services matrix

in line. Once they achieve this and IT resources are more closely aligned with the needs and demands of the business units, they would move to the top right quadrant. The number of management accountants working in large IT departments is growing every year, and working towards a position in this top right quadrant should be one of their primary objectives. Getting there will bring substantial benefits to their organization.

8

Assessing the Return on
Investing in Budgeting

Considering planning and budgeting is one of the few truly enterprise-wide processes, it is remarkable how little the cost of it is scrutinized. Large organizations continue to use spreadsheets for budgeting in the belief that they are a cheap option as they come almost free of charge on standard desktop software. This shortsighted thinking fails to take account of the immense amount of time that both the finance team and the individual responsibility centre managers invest in planning and budgeting. For example, one study[1] found that inefficient budgeting consumed between 20 and 30% of senior management time. An oft-quoted study by The Hackett Group, a consulting organization specializing in benchmarking, revealed that a company with $1 billion in revenues typically spends 25 000 man-days per year on planning, budgeting and measuring performance. Reducing this translates into some realisable cost savings, most likely by reducing the resource requirements in the finance team previously used to manipulate a myriad of spreadsheets, as well as a significant increase in management time that could be better used on initiatives that will create value.

Calculating the tangible benefits

The first challenge when assessing the return to be had from investing in planning and budgeting is to quantify the tangible benefits that come from simply making the planning and budgeting process more efficient. This should be tackled in exactly the same way as any other investment in process improvement, such as implementing an expense management system, automating a production process or deploying a document imaging and retrieval system. That means capturing the direct and indirect cost of the entire process and comparing the costs before and after the implementation.

As an example, we will adopt the accepted approach to investment appraisal using a net present value (NPV), approach over a 5-year period. This is a typical period used for a capital expenditure appraisal for software, although in many instances the cost of software is only a small proportion of the overall spend. A NPV calculation considers a set of cash flows over a number of years and discounts them back to their present value. This takes into account the reality that an amount of money today is worth more than the same amount at some distant point of time in the future. One reason for this is because you have access to the money today and can invest it to generate interest in the future. Consider investing £100 over a period of 5 years at a fixed interest rate of 10%. By the end of Year 5, this investment will have risen to £161.05. But given that you would have to wait for 5 years, the NPV of that £161.05 today is actually £100.

The cash flows in our ROI appraisal occur at different times. In the first year, we have to spend heavily to acquire and implement the software. But the cost savings go on indefinitely. So the only way we can access whether the investment is worthwhile is to establish a suitable timescale and discount all the cash flows that occur during that period back to their net present values. The value of future cash flows at any future date can be translated back to their present value by applying the discount rate or interest rate prevailing at the time. This can be represented by the following formula:

$$\text{NPV} = S^0 - E^0 + \{S^1 - E^1\}/\{1 - r\} + \{S^2 - E^2\}/\{1 - r^2\} \cdots \{S^n - E^n\}/\{1 - r^n\}$$

where

NPV $=$ net present value
$S^i =$ cost savings received in year i
$E^i =$ expenses incurred in year i
$r =$ the rate of interest or discount rate used for the cash flows
$n =$ the number of years used for the appraisal

Most people grasp the logic that underpins NPV quickly with the most common question being how to decide what discount rate to use. At its simplest, the discount rate should be the rate of return that those who supply funds to the company require for making an investment with this level of risk. If they could get a better return with an equivalent level of risk or a similar level of return at a lower risk, they would invest elsewhere. An investor can achieve a risk-free rate of return by depositing their money in a bank and sets the absolute lower limit for any discount rate. The appropriate rate to use in any investment appraisal depends on the risk profile of the particular company (more mature business with more consistent cash flows having less risk than start-ups in volatile markets), as well as on the way in which the business secures funding. Public companies fund their activities from both equities and debt. In such situations, the appropriate rate of discount to use is called the weighted average cost of capital (WACC), which takes into account the way funds are being provided, the rate of return that shareholders and banks require and the rate of corporation tax in that debt financing effectively reduces tax liability. The WACC is the sum of the after-tax rate of return on debt multiplied by the proportion of debt in the company's overall funding and the rate of return on equity multiplied by the proportion of equity in the company's overall funding. This can be represented by the following formula:

$$\text{WACC} = (1-t)r^{d} \times D/(D+E) + r^{e}E/(D+E)$$

where

$t =$ rate of corporation tax
$r^{d} =$ the rate of return required on debt financing
$r^{e} =$ the rate of return required on equity
$D =$ the value of debt financing in the company
$E =$ the value of equity financing in the company

Thankfully, you are not expected to work out a WACC yourself and doubtlessly your finance department will provide you with the right figure to use in your NPV calculation. If the outcome is positive, the investment generates positive cash flows and is worth doing unless any better investment opportunity exists. If the outcome is negative, the investment consumes cash and is not worth doing.

So what goes into the calculation?

Software and hardware costs

The largest and most obvious costs are those for planning and budgeting software and the servers it will run on. In addition to the one-off cost for licensing the software, you will need to include an allowance for annual maintenance charges (typically 20% and sometimes more). Similarly, when you include an annual cost for the depreciation of a new server needed for running the software, you should include the cost of any annual maintenance or support agreement that goes with it.

IT support

All IT applications need support and the cost of this should not be ignored. This means including a one-off cost to cover the initial installation and testing of the application, periodic costs to cover installing and testing new releases of the software, as well as the monthly cost of ongoing IT management and support. If your IT department has a well-developed system for reporting and cross-charging their services to the business, they will be able to provide you with fairly accurate assessment of what will be the current costs for each of these elements and you can simply increase these to reflect price inflation for the future years. In instances where the IT department has limited ability to report on its costs, you will probably have to rely on some rough and ready rules of thumb to arrive at these figures, factoring the amount of man-days involved in each activity and the average cost of a man-day.

It is increasing common for organizations to outsource part or all of their IT function to a third party provider. If this is the case, you may need to provide your supplier with a detailed specification of what is involved in installing, maintaining and supporting your application so they can provide you with an estimate of the costs involved. Some IT outsourcing agreements are provided as fixed price contracts. If this is the case, you will need to ensure whether your new application is covered by the existing agreement and when the existing agreement ends. Doing this upfront will preclude the surprise of unanticipated expenses at some point in the future.

Do not forget to include any savings that may result from decommissioning any existing planning and budgeting application. These could include savings from cancelling annual maintenance agreements and savings from decommissioning redundant servers.

Initial implementation

Unless you systematically work through each of the elements involved, it is easy to underestimate the cost of the initial implementation. The checklist below shows the elements that are typically encountered when implementing a new planning and budgeting application, but you may uncover others:

- **Project management**

It is usual for somebody from inside the organization to spend a large part if not all of their time managing the project. Their involvement may start at the very early stages of identifying the organization's requirements and run through information gathering, preparing and reviewing requests for information, shortlisting and selecting vendors, right through to testing and rolling out the final solution. As such the amount of time they commit to the project may vary with time and this needs to be captured in your calculation.

- **Project team members**

In many instances, a project manager will be supported by a multi-disciplinary team made up of people from the finance and IT functions and representatives from the user community. The cost of their involvement in the project should also be reflected in your model.

- **Information gathering**

At the early stages of a project, organizations will typically review current thinking and best practice on planning and budgeting as a precursor to specifying their own requirements. There is a wealth of information that can be gleaned from the Internet and today one does not have to search far to find a plethora of published articles, white papers and web seminars. Although the information is free and quick to collect, it is not always objective and usually reflects the particular interests of a consulting organization, vendor or academic. During this exploratory stage, it is also important to be able to test out your ideas and clarify any areas of confusion. For these reasons, many project leaders will find attending external courses run by the accounting institutes very useful. Not only will you be exposed to the latest thinking, you will benefit from being able to test out your ideas with a recognized expert and a group of like-minded delegates.

Likewise, making sense of the marketing hype put out by software vendors may prove difficult, and project leaders may find it useful to purchase independent assessment reports from the leading IT analysts. For the sake of thoroughness, all of these costs should be included in your assessment.

- **External contractors**

Any implementation is likely to involve external resources. These include implementation services consultants provided by the software vendor to help install the software and build the budget model as well as independent consultants with more general expertise in helping organizations with managing change and improving their financial performance. Where an independent consultancy is retained, it is usual for one of their senior staff to take on the responsibility for project management.

- **Internal implementation expenses**

In addition to using your chosen vendor's implementation services team and possibly retaining an independent third-party consulting organization, most organizations will want to have their own staff actively involved in working with the new application. Usually this means having a few technically savvy management accountants help develop the planning and budgeting model or produce input screens and reports. Involving its own staff means that the organization will gain the skills and capability to maintain and amend the solution once the initial implementation is complete and the external contractors have disappeared off the scene. This will undoubtedly save costs in the future, but for the moment costs for both the amount of time these people spend on the project and for any specific training they receive beforehand should be added into the calculation.

Ongoing costs

Once the cost of acquiring and implementing the software has been identified, attention needs to turn to assessing the cost of the two core business processes, which for the sake of simplicity we will label "doing the annual budget" and "doing re-forecasting". Not every organization will have an annual budgeting process and not every organization will undertake an interim re-forecast, let alone practice monthly rolling re-forecasts. However, most organizations will find it easier to keep these two processes separate and run their ROI calculation on a before-and-after comparison of their current practice. So if your organization currently does an annual budget and two mid-year re-forecasts, you should base your ROI appraisal on that. You may wish to re-forecast more frequently in the future, but if you compare the cost of doing an annual budget and two mid-year re-forecasts with the cost of doing an annual budgeting and four mid-year re-forecasts, you are hardly comparing apples with apples.

Estimating the amount of time and cost that the organization spends on budgeting and re-forecasting is best achieved by adopting a simple empirical approach:

1. Identifying exactly who is involved in the two processes (e.g. the annual budgeting cycle, a mid-year re-forecast).
2. Group people with a similar type and level of involvement together. In practice this might result in four groups of people covering the following:
   - More junior management accounting staff directly involved in the budgeting process.
   - Senior management accounting and finance staff responsible for reviewing, approving and presenting budgets and re-forecasts.
   - Individual cost centre managers responsible for developing, preparing and submitting budgets.
   - Senior managers who review and approve cost centre manager's plans and budgets.
3. Estimate the amount of time that a member of each of the above groups typically spends on: (i) the annual planning and budgeting cycle and (ii) each round of re-forecasting. This can be expressed as the average

number of working days or, in the case of the management accountants, as a percentage of their entire working time.

4. Work with your finance department to establish a fully loaded daily cost for the salary and benefits of the average person in each of the above groups. Remember that accounting for holidays, in most organizations people work less than 230 days a year.

5. Use this fully laden daily cost to calculate the total cost of (i) doing the annual budget and (ii) doing a mid-year re-forecast.

6. The next step is to benchmark some improvements in the process. These can only take two forms. Either less people are involved in the two processes or, more likely, it takes the people less time to complete the process. In the worked example of Itzalot plc in Table 8.1, both the number of people involved (saving one junior management accountant) and the amount of time it takes others to prepare and submit their budgets and re-forecasts have been reduced.

7. Having estimated a new figure for the ongoing cost for the planning, budgeting and re-forecast, it is possible to identify the variance between the two results and take this into the NPV calculation, inflating it each year to account for the wage increases.

Worked example of estimating the organizational cost of budgeting and re-forecasting

What follows is a worked example for Itzalot plc, a company which anticipates investing in a new planning, budgeting and re-forecasting system. The costs of the initial implementation are set out in Table 8.3. These are relatively easy to estimate. The more difficult task is to estimate to cost of "doing" planning and budgeting at Itzalot. But if the above approach is used the result will be accurate enough for input into the NPV calculation and if anyone wishes to query the costs, it is always possible to review the underlying assumptions and recalculate the costs.

Itzalot plc starts kicking off its annual budgeting cycle during the first week of September and completes the process with the board approving the final submission during the last week of November, some fifteen weeks later. During this time, three junior management accountants spent 80% of their time fully involved in the process. The Budget Controller, who they report to, and the CFO reckon they spend a total of 20 days each involved in the budget at this busy time.

Table 8.1 Current cost of planning, budgeting and re-forecasting at Itzalot

Group	# Members	Average fully laden cost	Cost/working day	Annual budgeting cycle		Round of re-forecasting	
				# Days involvement	Cost	# Days involvement	Cost
	a	b	$c = b/220$	d	$e = d \times c \times a$	f	$g = f \times c \times a$
Junior management accountants	3	£37,500	£170.45	60	£30,682	9	£4,602
CFO and budgeting controller	2	£88,000	£400.00	20	£16,000	0.5	£400
Cost centre managers	45	£42,500	£193.18	9	£78,239	2	£17,386
Senior managers	15	£65,000	£295.45	5	£22,159	1	£4,432
Sub-total					£147,080		£26,820
# Times per year					1		2
Sub-total					£147,080		£53,640

The total budgeting and re-forecasting cost is £200,720.

Forty-five cost centre managers contribute to the budget and it is estimated that with reviews and resubmissions, they spend an average of 9 days a year working on the budget. In addition there are fifteen senior managers who take an average of five working days to review and approve budgets.

The company currently does two rounds of re-forecasts during its financial year. Each re-forecast takes 12 working days to complete and during this time the three junior management accountants spend 75% of their time involved in the process; their boss and the CFO spending only half a day to review the re-forecast once it is complete. It is estimated that preparing a re-forecast takes each cost centre manager two working days and that the fifteen senior managers spend a day each reviewing and approving the re-forecasts. All this information is brought together to provide the estimate of the current cost of planning, budgeting and re-forecasting which is shown in Table 8.1.

Having estimated the current cost of planning, budgeting and re-forecasting for Itzalot plc, we need to make some assumptions about the amount of time that will be saved once the new software is in use. After speaking with other companies already using the software, the project manager at Itzalot estimates that the saving will be as follows:

The Annual budgeting cycle

- Annual budget cycle reduced to 4 working weeks during which time 2 junior management accountants will be spend 60% of their time on the process.
- Involvement of CFO and Budget Controller reduced to 5 days.
- Cost centre managers involvement reduced to 3 days.
- Senior managers involvement reduced to 1 day.

Re-forecasting cycle

- A re-forecast now takes 5 working days to complete and during this time the two junior management accountants spend 50% of their time involved in the process.
- The CFO and the Budget Controller still spend half a day reviewing the re-forecast.
- Cost centre manager take only half a working day to re-forecast.
- The fifteen senior managers spend only half a day reviewing and approving the re-forecasts.

Table 8.2 shows the new total for the cost of planning, budgeting and re-forecasting within Itzalot plc.

Comparing these two estimates shows that implementing the new approach to planning and budgeting and the new software result in an annual saving of £146,488 (£200,720 – £54,232). This figure is made up of staff costs and would need to be inflated by the anticipated annual salary increase for it to be included in a net present value investment appraisal.

Now we have everything we need to complete the ROI calculation. We have identified the detailed costs of the implementation, estimated the annual cost savings from having a quicker and more efficient budgeting and forecasting system, and have been provided with a figure for cost of capital by the finance department. It is simply a matter of building a simple spreadsheet model, slot in the expenses or savings in the years they occur and write a rule to discount them all to their net present value. Table 8.3 shows how this information is brought together with the cost of the initial implementation to complete the NPV calculation for Itzalot.

Implementing the new planning and budgeting system costs £268 300 and has ongoing costs in future years. But the calculation shows a positive result of £270,901 which means the investment is worth doing and breaks even early in Year 2.

You may think the NPV appraisal above to be a long-winded and possibly pointless exercise based on speculative cost savings. But consider it from the perspective of a board member being asked to approve expenditure of over a quarter of million pounds. They may support the project, seeing the value of being able to budget quicker and re-forecast more frequently. But if you provide them with some quantified measure of the value of the investment, they will be able to state their case more convincingly and you stand a better chance of securing board approval for the implementation. On the other hand, if you present a proposal for the project without a quantified ROI, it is all too easy for a cynical board member to dismiss the project. So do not underestimate the value of an ROI appraisal. Even those asking for multimillion pounds worth of investment are based on estimates of the future size and growth of markets that today are either non-existent or embryonic. The inputs are always far more important than the actual methodology, and you should always document how you estimated the annual cost savings and provide a range of assessments showing a best, worst and most likely scenario. Board members may well be astounded to learn that it takes their company months to complete an annual

Table 8.2 Forecast cost of planning, budgeting and re-forecasting at Itzalot

Group	# Members	Average fully laden cost	Cost/working day	Annual budgeting cycle		Round of re-forecasting	
				# Days involvement	Cost	# Days involvement	Cost
	a	b	$c = b/220$	d	$e = d \times c \times a$	f	$g = f \times c \times a$
Junior management accountants	2	£37,500	£170.45	12	£4,091	2.5	£852
CFO and budgeting controller	2	£88,000	£400.00	5	£4,000	0.5	£400
Cost centre managers	45	£42,500	£193.18	3	£26,080	0.5	£4,347
Senior managers	15	£65,000	£295.45	1	£4,432	0.5	£2,216
Sub-total					£38,603		£7,815
# Times per year					1		2
Sub-total					£38,603		£15,630

The total budgeting and re-forecasting cost is £54,233.

Table 8.3 Worked example of an ROI calculation using net present value (in £)

		Year 0	Year 1	Year 2	Year 3	Year 4	
Investment							
Software, Hardware & IT Support							
Software	a	85,000					
Software Maintenance Agreement	b	17,000	17,000	17,000	17,000	17,000	
Hardware	c	24,000					
Hardware Service Agreement	d	4,800	4,800	4,800	4,800	4,800	
Internal IT Support	e	34,500	15,000	15,450	15,914	16,391	
Implementation							
Training	f	12,500					
External Consulting Services	g	30,000					
Internal project management	h	24,500					
Internal Implementation team	i	36,000					
Sub-total	$j = Sum(a \ldots i)$	268,300	36,800	37,250	37,714	38,191	
Cost savings							
Annual cost saving	k		146,488	150,883	155,409	160,071	164,874
Net Cash Flows	$l = k - j$	(121,812)	114,083	118,159	122,358	126,683	
NPV Calculation							
Discount rate used	8.50%						
Year 4						126,683	
Year 3					122,358	116,758	
Year 2				118,159	112,772	107,611	
Year 1			114,083	108,902	103,938	99,181	
Year 0		(121,812)	105,145	100,371	95,795	91,411	270,910

budget and are unable to re-forecast with the frequency that is required in business today. Try to think of your project proposal as a sales document that addresses the interests and concerns of its audience. You want them to buy into the idea and approve the expenditure, so ensure you include everything that makes that decision easy.

Accessing the intangible benefits

Once the investment appraisal has been reviewed, the attention of those tasked with approving or rejecting your project will quickly turn to the more intangible benefits such as agility, alignment and better visibility into the future. These are the real reasons for needing to invest in a new planning and budgeting system and you should spend as much, if not more, time on preparing the business case around these issues as you did preparing the NPV appraisal.

There is a tendency to talk about these issues in an abstract manner under the heading of "business transformation". However, there are undoubted benefits to be had from defining exactly what you mean by terms such as "agility" or "alignment", describing how it is dealt with inside your organization today, how long it takes – and how you envisage it once the new system is implemented. Doing this enable directors and senior management to fully understand why such issues are important, how they will be transformed and the benefits this will bring. For example:

Definition

"Alignment" is defined as the ability of the organization to quickly realign controllable costs so that each department has the optimal amount of capacity to deal with the demands being placed on it. Excess capacity is a wasted resource and this negatively impacts profitability.

Current situation

One of the key performance indicators inside the organization is customer retention, which is currently measured by comparing the number of active trading accounts at the end of each month. Typically this runs at between 94 and 96%, the parameters deemed to be acceptable being set in the corporate dashboard at 92.5 and 97.5%. However, minor changes in the number of active trading accounts and the average number of orders they place each month has sufficient impact on the demands placed on certain departments such as the sales office and the pick and pack operation that every month they ought to review their staffing.

As it currently takes the company more than two weeks to complete a mid-year re-forecast, there is only one re-forecast during the financial year. This exercise is very beneficial. Analysis has shown that during the first few months of each half year, staffing is tightly aligned with demand with little or no excess capacity in these departments. However the situation in the last three months of each quarter is far from satisfactory with departments in some regions being over-staffed and others understaffed. Both overstaffing and understaffing damages our financial performance. During the second quarter of this year, our analysis identified £25,800 worth of excess capacity in these two departments, even when a buffer of 10% was applied to optimal staffing levels to accommodate daily fluctuations in order levels. The converse of this is that understaffing in these departments delays despatch and results in higher levels of customer dissatis-faction and a subsequent decrease in customer retention levels in subsequent months. Region 2 suffered badly from understaffing at the end of last year and it is estimated that this resulted in the £820,000 of lost sales and £48,000 of lost profit.

Desired future

Implementing the new planning and budgeting system will enable the company to move to monthly rolling re-forecasts constantly looking forward 18 months. Key account managers and regional sales managers will start the process on the first Monday of each month by updating their sales forecasts. A simulation has shown this will take them approximately half a day. After this, the key operational departments such as the sales office and the pick and pack operation can quickly review their staffing requirements and complete their re-forecast. This will be done by the end of the following day.

The net result is that any temporary staff employed during the previous month can be let go at the end of the week. Today this rarely happens as managers have no idea of the sales forecast and always tend to err on the side of caution. Alternatively where they are facing increased demand, managers can place their standard recruitment advertisements in the local weekly papers that o to press on Wednesday evenings.

While it is difficult to precisely quantify the business benefits, we have set our-selves the goal of managing capacity so that it is as good as, if not better than, that which we currently achieve in the first month of each half year. We esti-mate this to save over £90,000 in annual staffing costs in these two departments alone.

What we have tried to do in this example is to make the intangible tangible. First, we have defined what we mean by "alignment" to ensure a common understanding. Then, we have described the process as it presently manifests itself, identifying the problems this causes in the business. Finally, we have to set out alternative future with a new planning and budgeting process and a new system. Few could disagree with such a compelling business case.

Summary

Enthusiasm alone will never win the day. Senior managers and their boards need to be convinced that any investment in new planning and budgeting systems is going to bring benefits. Some of these benefits will be tangible (and perhaps even bankable), while others, like agility, will be less tangible. If a systematic approach is taken to assessing the cost of the implementation and perhaps more importantly the ongoing cost of budgeting and forecasting, it is possible to build a compelling business case for adopting a driver-based approach to planning and budgeting. But ROI appraisal does not end as soon as approval has been granted. There should be a number of post-implementation reviews to check whether the forecast cost savings were realized, and if not, why not.

Note

1   O'Connell, B., "Beyond Budgeting & Forecasting: New Tools, Strategies Making an Old Job Easier", *Business Finance Magazine*, January 2001.

Systems Requirements for Supporting Driver-Based Budgeting

Any budget controller or a management accountant inside an organization that uses spreadsheets for enterprise budgeting will spend a significant amount of time and effort every year valiantly battling their way through the budgeting process and may think that going straight into a discussion about the type of system needed to implement driver-based budgeting is not addressing their immediate needs. It would be like asking a dehydrated man lost in a desert whether he wanted still or sparkling water as he crawled into the oasis. For the moment, anything might seem preferable to what they currently have. However, if they have even the germ of an idea of moving towards a driver-based approach to planning and budgeting in the short to medium term, they need to ensure that the budgeting system they buy or build today to satisfy their current pain points provides the functionality they will need in the future. Most enterprise applications have a life of between 7 and 8 years before they are decommissioned and replaced. So asking for another new budgeting system within a couple of years of the last one could be a career limiting move that is best avoided, unless there is an opportunity to follow the advice set out in the previous chapter and build a compelling business case and ROI for the type of budgeting system they now seek. At the same time there is an increasing number of people who would like to implement driver-based budgeting but find themselves lumbered with a budgeting system their predecessor implemented not so long ago. They too will have to patiently sit on their hands for a few years – or set about building an equally compelling business case and return on investment.

To help avoid the short-term decision making that results in organizations selecting a system today that they might regret in the future, the system requirements of planning and budgeting systems have been split into two:

1. Characteristics that are needed to ensure that the finance department's current pain points are addressed.
2. Characteristics that are essential to support a driver-based approach to planning and budgeting.

Common characteristics of packaged budgeting applications

Packaged budgeting applications possess a number of characteristics that make them a better choice than spreadsheets for budgeting in larger organizations. They include the following:

- Pre-defined structures

By having pre-defined multidimensional hierarchies, packaged budgeting applications make it easy to add new departments, products, periods and line items without significant manipulation of consolidation processes, data entry screens or reports.

- Data management tools

Administrators need easy-to-use systems that allow them to import and export data. This helps them export a completed budget to their financial systems and import actual expense from the general ledger for period-end variance reporting. Once configured, these links can be automated for use in future periods.

- Automatic consolidation

Consolidation is automatic, and unless overridden, follows the default path of the defined hierarchies. Any new department, product or line item simply consolidates with the others at the particular point it is added in the structure.

- Versioning

Systems administrators can quickly create new versions of a budget for a re-forecast, new budget year or scenario. Once done, a version can be made current so that is the only version that users are able to amend. Versions can also be locked so that users can make no further changes.

- Security

Administrators can control users' access to the budgeting system and limit their ability to view and change certain pieces of data. Most organizations limit a user's access to their own data and that of their subordinates. Today, many large organizations prefer budgeting systems that offer a "single sign-on" so that users are automatically assigned the same username and password they use when logging in to their organization's network.

- International capabilities

Contributors can enter data in their local currency into screens that use their local language with both budgeted and actual expenses being converted into a common currency at exchange rates controlled by the system administrator.

- Annotation

Contributors can add notes and narratives against individual pieces or ranges of data that others can refer to. This is useful when explaining their assumptions or the reasons for any changes between versions.

- Web-based data entry and reporting

Most budgeting applications allow users to input data and view reports over a local area network or the web. This means that a new budgeting system can be rapidly deployed to a large community of contributors in any location without having to pre-install software on individual's desktops. This is not to say that there is no software on users' desktop PCs. In some instances, a small calculation engine is automatically downloaded over the web and users are able to recalculate their departmental budget on their desktop.

- Audit trails

As publicly quoted companies move towards forward-looking statements about future earnings, they will want the same level of audit trails they have in other financial reporting systems; that is to be able to identify the current and previous value of any piece of data that has been changed together with exact details of who changed it and when.

- Data entry wizards

Many applications will have a selection of pre-built functions to accelerate data entry. For instance, inputting "12 @2000" in the first cell of any line item will typically populate each cell from January to December with the value 2000.

- Workflow Management

Coordinating a large community of contributors to deliver a budget or re-forecast to a tight deadline is not easy. A workflow management tool allows an administrator to schedule the budget submission and authorization process, automatically sending out e-mails to trigger the process, alert any laggards and their managers of upcoming deadlines and monitor an individual's progress. Once configured, a workflow routine can be called upon repeatedly, so that it is always available to help expedite rolling re-forecasts.

It is likely that anyone currently battling with spreadsheets will find many of their current bugbears addressed by the functionality listed above. However, not all enterprise planning and budgeting software supports driver-based budgeting. So if the intention is to adopt a driver-based approach to planning and budgeting from the outset, or to migrate towards it at some point in the future, care needs to be taken to ensure that the budgeting package chosen is capable of supporting it.

Specific software characteristics for driver-based budgeting

There are a small number of specific bits of functionality that any planning and budgeting application must have in order to support driver-based planning and budgeting:

- Writing rules

Driver-based budgeting relies on being able to write rules and formulas. This is something that many enterprise planning and budgeting applications offer to some degree. Almost all allow enterprise-wide rules to be written for certain line items, such as the line item expense for postage is always the number of items mailed multiplied by the second-class stamp rate regardless of department, period or version. Most will also allow rules to be written between line items and periods within a department. For instance, if 80% of new policy applications received in an underwriting department during the current period are processed in the current period and 20% in the following period, then we need to create a rule to calculate the actual number processed in any period.

But few are capable of handling rules that cross departments, such as where the number of pieces of direct mail issued by marketing creates inbound sales calls into a customer contact centre that in turn creates new business sales that need to be fulfilled by operations, and finally results in an item of outbound post to be despatched by the mail room. If you follow that process through from end to end, with the output of one department becoming the input of the next, there are a string of rules that span each of the four departments involved. Most enterprise planning and budgeting systems cannot easily handle this. Rather than having users entering data into a single central database, most budgeting systems work by downloading a subset of the data to the users' desktop. Then once individual contributors have prepared their submissions, the separate data elements are collected and the model is calculated to generate the consolidated result. This means that each time there is a rule that crosses a department, the separate data elements have to be collected and the model recalculated. In the example above, the model would need to be reconsolidated and recalculated three times: first to make the rule between the marketing department and the contact centre work; then to make the rule between the contact centre and operations work; and finally to make the rule between operations and the post-room work. The amount of time and effort in doing this negates much of the benefits of driver-based budgeting.

To implement driver-based planning and budgeting, organizations need an application that allows users to enter data directly into a central database and does not download separate data elements down to desktops. That way, whenever a user changes a piece of data that impacts a department downstream of them, as soon as the model is refreshed and recalculated the downstream user has access to the new data. In practice, a work management tool is used to schedule users' submissions along the value chain and using this approach organizations are delivering enterprise-wide, driver-based rolling re-forecasts every month with individual users spending no more then 10–15 minutes reviewing and amending their departmental forecasts.

- Calculation

For driver-based planning and budgeting to be easy to implement, individual users need to be able to change any piece of data and recalculate the results for the part of the model they are currently viewing. So if a fleet manager decides to change their forecast for the price of fuel in a future period, they need the facility to trigger a recalculation of their departmental budget. In fact as they test out various assumptions they may wish to recalculate their departmental budget many times until they are satisfied with the overall result and ready to submit it. This is exactly the same process which cost centre managers go through when they model off-line on spreadsheets in a traditional budgeting environment and any system used for driver-based planning and budgeting needs to offer the same functionality with similar response times. If it fails to do this, it will have failed in the eyes of the users.

Similarly when any other user opens a view, the software should automatically calculate all the current results for every line item in the view. So, for instance, if the budget administrator opens a report showing a cash flow statement, the software should automatically calculate the impact of all the recent changes, including the fact that the fleet manager forecasts that the price of fuel will increase in Period 10.

In effect, whenever there is a change to any piece of data, the system needs to detect it and deal with it in an appropriate manner. If a user has asked for their view to be recalculated or a new user has opened a view where all the line items are not yet fully calculated, those should be given priority. Otherwise the calculation engine should be constantly vigilant to any uncalculated results and be steadily working away at calculating them until there is nothing else for it to do.

This type of calculation process is completely at odds with those in a traditional planning and budgeting application, where other than those departmental calculations done on the desktop, consolidated results are not produced until the very end of the process. Because of this, the type of server needed to run software for driver-based planning and budgeting needs to be more powerful than that typically used for traditional planning and budgeting. Calculation needs to be both on-demand and rapid.

However, just because there might be a few hundred cost centre managers who contribute to the budget, does not mean that driver-based budgeting needs unlimited computing power to guarantee satisfactory response times every time a calculation is triggered. Driver-based planning and budgeting is built around horizontal business processes so that a departmental manager cannot commence their own planning and budgeting until the person upstream of them has submitted theirs; the mail room manager has to wait for operations; operations has to wait for the customer contact centre; the customer contact centre has to wait for the marketing department. And none of the support functions such as IT can start planning and budgeting until these front-line departments have finished. Again workflow management tools help expedite this process, but at any one time there will be only a subset of the total number of users working with the system.

At this point you may well be thinking that you could easily implement driver-based planning and budgeting using spreadsheets so why would you need to implement a packaged budgeting application? This is a valid observation. My first encounter with a comprehensive driver-based planning and budgeting model was built using a spreadsheet package. It was in an express delivery company, and managers at each collection and delivery depot completed their annual budget schedule by entering driver volumes, such as the number of active customers each period, the number of shipments each type of customer would ship every day, the average weight of each shipment and the revenue per shipped kilogram. Entering these values drove most of the depot's resource requirements and line item expenses and for a multi-site operation, this was an effective way of budgeting that reflected the way the depot managers understood and managed their business on a day-to-day basis. Nobody called it driver-based budgeting or considered it to be anything special. It was just their way they did things in that business. It made sense and it worked. However, all the support functions still used traditional budgeting and consolidating a multitude of spreadsheets was still an unwieldy and error-prone task. So although it is possible to build a driver-based planning and budgeting model around spreadsheets, if there is a large number of contributors, organizations are likely to encounter some of the familiar problems that have already been documented. Spreadsheets are ideal tools for developing pilot studies in a couple of departments to get management buy-in to the concept and to demonstrate some of the benefits. But when it comes to a large-scale implementation, they are best abandoned for a purpose-built package.

Figure 9.1 combines these two criteria and diagrammatically shows where the ideal solution for implementing driver-based planning and budgeting is likely to be found. The vertical axis, which has been labelled "Efficiency for Budgeting" represents all the core functionality, such as versioning, workflow and automatic consolidation that will address many of the finance department's immediate pain points. The horizontal axis labelled "Suitability for Driver-Based Planning and Budgeting" represents the functionality that is critical to support driver-based budgeting, such as inter-departmental rules and on-demand calculation.

However there is a halfway house between packaged budgeting solutions and spreadsheets in that a number of products use standard spreadsheets as

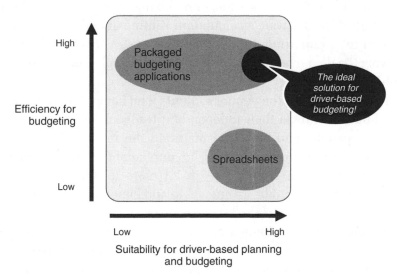

Figure 9.1 The ideal solution for implementing driver-based planning and budgeting

the primary user interface and some other vendors offer it as an optional user interface. As long as all the rules and assumptions used in the enterprise driver-based planning and budgeting model are not left on the desktop, this is a happy medium and provides users with the familiar spreadsheet look and feel.

Somewhere in the plethora of packaged planning and budgeting applications organizations will find a solution capable of delivering the functionality they need. However, there are some guidelines that will help in the search for the right software:

- Identify the most complex rule or relationship in your model and provide your shortlisted software vendors with some sample data to enable them to build a small proof of concept model that incorporates this rule. Get them to build this model on your site with you and your colleagues present. You should be comfortable that the vendor can build the model quickly and efficiently and that you already have or can quickly acquire the skills required for writing rules yourself. Ultimately you need to be able to build and maintain you budget model yourselves and it is unlikely that you will be able to do this if rules are written in some arcane and highly specialized scripting language.
- Specifically test the capability of the software to support the rules that cross departments. Get the vendor to open a view for a specified depart-ment and change a number that has an impact on another downstream department. Then get them to immediate open a view for the second department so you can see the same changed number. This test gets to the heart of the software's calculation routine and shows whether it will support inter-department rules. Needless to say, this test should be done viewing the data over the web rather than through a power user or model builder interface.
- Contact a number of the vendor's clients who have implemented a driver-based budget and get their independent feedback. If you can, try to meet with the people who built and maintain the model as well as some of the users. As you are intending to implement a similar type of bud-geting process, you should have a lot more to discuss other than the software and it should be an enjoyable and beneficial experience for both of you.
- Understand how the budgeting software integrates with other systems and see it in operation. There are the obvious imports and exports of line item expenses from the finance systems, but you may wish to upload data directly from specific operational planning applications in areas

such as marketing, the customer contact centre and operations. How far you decide to go in integrating these types of domain specific applications is a trade-off between the amount of effort involved in creating and maintaining a uni-directional, or perhaps even a bi-directional, link and the amount of data being transferred. If all that is involved is a few line item expenses, it may be easier simply to re-key them.

Integration with other performance management applications

Many of the drivers that will be at the core of any driver-based planning and budgeting model will be central to other performance applications also. They are as follows:

- Key performance indicators that would populate one of the perspectives of a balanced scorecard.
- Important resource drivers or activity drivers that would be used in an ABC model used for reporting the costs and profitability of customers, products and distribution channels, costing core business processes and costing shared services for cross-charging them back to the front-line business units.

This leads to the inevitable conclusion that budgeting, costing and scorecarding applications should not longer be stand-alone or point solutions. They should be part of a suite that shares a single database and a common user interface. That way when any piece of data is changed, it is immediately available for use in the other applications. Despite the lack of legislation, there is increasing pressure on publicly listed companies to provide investors, potential investors and other stakeholders, such as employees, with guidance on how changes in their external or internal environment are expected to impact future profitability. This brings financial consolidation into the equation. Preparing statutory accounts according to various accepted accounting practices is normally done at some remote corporate head office by financial accountants whose only interest has been historic data. But they too could soon be interested in forecasting and modelling the impact that changing drivers have on future earnings. And if company boards and their external auditors ever have to formally sign off these forward-looking statements, there will undoubtedly be a high level of interest in understanding the way in which the business units came up with the forecast. Planning and budgeting methodologies may well become an agenda item at board meetings.

None of these four financial management methodologies (budgeting, costing, scorecarding and financial consolidation) is new, and many organizations will have many if not all of them already implemented. However, in most instances they will be deployed as stand-alone systems each with their own user interface and separate database. What is now being suggested is that they become part of an integrated suite of applications, something that has been labelled "corporate performance management" or CPM for short. The term is used to describe the processes involved in managing financial and non-financial performance – such as formulating strategy, allocating resources, and managing costs and profitability; the methodologies that underpin some of these processes – such as the balanced scorecard, budgeting and ABC; and the metrics and data used to manage these processes.

Since CPM was first defined in 2001, the term or some near variant, such as "business performance management" (BPM) or "enterprise performance management" (EPM) has been adopted by numerous software vendors who have broadened their existing range of applications either by developing additional applications themselves or by acquiring smaller vendors. This has resulted in vendors offering some or all of the application areas listed above. However, few vendors can claim to have a CPM suite as much of the functionality is still offered as separate applications each with its own user interface and database. This compromises the ability of the user to move seamlessly between methodologies such as when changing a driver, such as the productivity of departmental staff which is a key piece of data in both a driver-based planning and budgeting model and a scorecard. Because the separate methodologies are not integrated there are also likely to be issues with metadata so that users may be dealing with differing definitions of specific pieces of data in each method-ology. In most instances, data is not shared across the methodologies; at best it is copied between the various applications creating issues with version control.

Figure 9.2 shows the fundamental systems' architecture that needs to underpin a suite of corporate performance management applications.

Note that the four methodologies share a single database and have a common user interface. This means that once a user changes any piece of data, the changed data is immediately available in any performance management model in the entire suite. Drivers have an important place in any CPM suite. Together with the core financial data, they form the glue that holds together planning and budgeting, ABC, scorecards and ultimately forward-looking statements of financial performance that look set to become an integral part of external reporting.

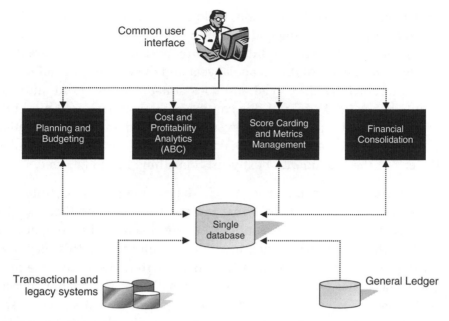

Figure 9.2 Fundamental architecture of any corporate performance management suite

Working life with fully enabled CPM

Michael is a business manager in an insurance company. He always starts his day by logging on the network. An alert in his inbox provides a hyperlink to his business unit's main scorecard where he sees an indicator for customer retention has recently moved from green to amber. He clicks on the indicator to reveal a table showing the underlying data. This shows that last month only 65% of the policyholders renewed their annual policy. This is a big drop over previous periods, which had been running consistently between 71 and 73%. He notices that someone has added a comment against the most recent entry. It is from Elaine in the customer contact centre suggesting that a competitor has been aggressively targeting the company's policyholders in the weeks preceding their renewal offering big discounts. He rings Elaine and asks her to review a sample of call logs for customers who have rung in to cancel their policy in the last few weeks and provide him with some comparisons. By lunch Michael gets an e-mail from Elaine suggesting that the discounts were typically between 5 and 10 % below what their renewal premium would have been.

After a quick lunch, Michael decides to do some scenario modelling, clicks into the enterprise planning and budgeting system and opens up a view showing the revenue forecast. Initially he reduces the customer retention rate to 65% for the rest of this financial year and the whole of the following year. He recalculates the model and goes straight to the profit and loss account. Just as he thought, if this continues the company will miss this year's profit target and next year revenue will fall dramatically. A quick click back to the scorecard shows that market share would start to tumble at the end of the first quarter next year. Something has to be done.

Reducing renewal premiums to match the competitors is definitely a non-starter. But Michael figures that temporarily reducing them by 5% for a period of four or five months is likely to make the competitor's assault on their customers much less effective and thinks this may lead them to drop it before the end of the third quarter. He sends an e-mail to the head actuary and asks her to see whether it is a viable sugges- tion. Michael meets her in the car park the next morning, when she tells him that her modelling suggests that it is affordable if the policy excess is increased slightly to compensate. But overall, she is confident and has already amended the premium, the forecast claims frequency and the cost of claims in the budgeting system. When he gets to his desk, Michael opens up a view of the newly re-forecast profit and loss account. It is nearly back to the original target, but it would be better to be safe than sorry. He opens up a cost and profitability report and sees that although the actual unit costs of the key business processes have been fairly stable, the recent downturn in the policy renewal rate has caused some of them to increase in the coming months and they are unlikely to recover until the very end of the year. Perhaps something could be done in the main processing departments to bring these unit costs back into line quicker.

He telephones Brian, the Head of Operations, and explains the situation. Brian quickly tells him that he is aware of the situation and that he can explain the reasons behind it. First, during the last couple of months there has been an abnormally high level of inbound service calls into the cus- tomer contact centre and he has had to recruite temporary staff to handle these. They chuckle as they realized this was due to current customers ringing in to cancel their policies and that they can now let these staff go. Then there is the lease on the additional floor space that he has been pressuring the landlord to make available from October onwards. Michael suggests that given the current situation, the company is unlikely to need this extra space until a month or so later than originally anticipated. Brian says that he will get his managers together to explain the revised plan and ask them to do a re-forecast. By the end of the day, it is done.

Michael checks the activity unit rates in a cost and profitability view and is pleased to see that they now show a much quicker recovery. They are nearly as good as they were earlier in the year. He then takes a look at the scorecard for Brian's part of the business. The new targets for all the KPIs are in place and Brian has added a commentary in the action plan to explain exactly what lays behind his latest re-forecast.

There is one last thing to do. Michael writes an e-mail to the Financial Controller at group head office and explains that his division's results for the third quarter will be a couple of per cent behind plan, but that it will be more than made up by the last quarter. He also reassures him that he is still confident that the division can achieve their long range forecast for the next twenty-four months. Michael knows that he will get an immediate reply thanking him for the update. There have been few surprises since the new system was put in, and they seem to like it that way.

Order of implementation for integrated solutions based on drivers

As organizations work towards integrating the various performance management methodologies into a single CPM solution around a single database, they are inevitably faced with the decision about where to start. While it is evident that activity-based budgeting cannot be implemented before activity-based costing, experience in numerous implementations suggests it makes little difference whether organizations start with activity-based costing or driver-based budgeting:

- Where a balanced scorecard has been built around a strategy map and the organization has clearly mapped what it needs to achieve to be financially successful, it should endeavour to use the KPIs that it has already identified as the starting point for developing a driver-based planning and budgeting model, or indeed any other aspect of CPM. If you do not start with strategy, where else do you start? Otherwise the famous

Lewis Carroll quotation from Alice in Wonderland comes to mind "If you don't know where you are going, any road will take you there".

- Where ABC models already exist, the organization may wish to leverage these to deliver activity-based budgeting and top–down scenario planning where this is a requirement. Then driver-based budgeting can be deployed for operational planning and budgeting, revealing any potential planning gap that may need to be filled with other strategic initiatives. Alternatively, the organization may decide to forego activity-based budgeting and simply implement driver-based planning and budgeting using the considerable insight about what drives costs to build the planning and budgeting model.

- In situations where there are no ABC models, it makes sense to start with the functionality that will deliver most benefit to the organization. Sometimes this will mean starting with ABC; sometimes this will mean starting with driver-based budgeting. There are many successful implementations that have followed both routes.

Faced with the incontrovertible logic that leads towards integrated corporate performance management suites, it would be shortsighted to implement any methodology without considering what other methodologies the organization currently has deployed or may wish to deploy in the future and how these will be delivered. If the organization has not yet developed such a long-term vision, it would be wise to spend time seeking external advice from consultants and IT analysts.

Summary

Software for supporting driver-based budgeting must fulfil two sets of criteria. First, it needs to make the budgeting process easier and more efficient addressing many of the immediate requirements of today's overstretched finance teams. But critically, it needs key pieces of functionality in order to fully support a driver-based approach. These are the ability to handle inter-departmental rules and an on-demand calculation engine that automatically recognizes when and where there are new results to recalculate. These two requirements should be included in any requests for information sent to software suppliers and be systematically tested during the software evaluation stage.

Implementing
Driver-Based Budgeting

Although this chapter has been called "Implementing Driver-Based Budgeting", it goes far beyond simply selecting and implementing software. Implementation itself starts at the very beginning of a project management cycle with clarifying and defining the emerging business need, goes through the planning and implementation stages, and finishes with project completion and ongoing maintenance. Along the way there will be a number of distinct stages, such as developing a pilot study, preparing the investment appraisal and selecting software.

Getting driver-based budgeting on the corporate agenda

However there is an important precursor to implementation – and that is getting driver-based budgeting on the corporate agenda for a start and this is shown in the stages of an implementation shown in Figure 10.1.

Sometimes this requires little in the way of planning and active intervention. The organization will have identified the need to improve its planning and

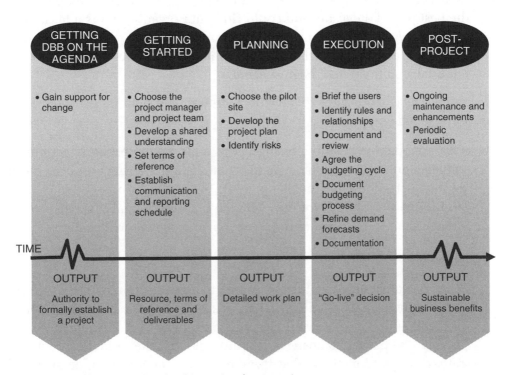

Figure 10.1 The stages involved in an implementation

budgeting process; someone will mention incorporating non-financial drivers to model certain resource requirements and line item expenses and the suggestion is immediately adopted. This often happens after the individual commissioned with coming up with suggestions to improve the budgeting process has done some research, read some books or attended a seminar and realized the benefits that adopting driver-based budgeting could bring to their organization. In other instances, another business division or even a competitor may have success-fully implemented it or perhaps the organization has recently been involved in a business process management, six sigma or ABC exercise, and realized the pervasiveness of operational drivers.

But not all organizations embrace driver-based budgeting with open arms – even when it is well suited to their particular situation. Someone, like you, who has taken the time to investigate the concept, will propose it as the answer to quicker budgeting and more frequent re-forecasting only to have their sugges-tion dismissed. Typically the reason give is either that it is "too complicated" or that "the business isn't ready for it yet". To date, few organizations have adopted driver-based planning and budgeting, but if you sit around and wait until it becomes mainstream, something the global IT analysts predict could take the best part of a decade, you could find your organization is a laggard or a late adopter while your competitors steal a march on you. So if you are sold on the concept and the benefits it brings, it is down to you to champion the cause and take on the role of change agent.

So the first piece of advice is to develop a strategy and plan for getting driver-based budgeting accepted.

- Use a model for business change. The most common one is set out in the equation below which suggests that change is a function of D (level of dissatisfaction with the status quo), V (the vision of a better future), and S (the first steps towards achieving that future) and this needs to be greater than R (the level of resistance) before change will occur:

  $$\text{Change} = f(D \times V \times S) > R$$

  Your role as change agent is to maximize dissatisfaction with the current process, paint a compelling vision of a better future and map a series of credible first steps towards its realization while simultaneously mini-mizing internal resistance. You should note that the formula is factorial rather than arithmetic so that if either of D, V or S is zero, change will never happen. You need to plan on all fronts. Develop a set of materials that address D, V and S. These can be positioning papers and presentations that set out the current problems with the planning and budgeting inside the organization today and how these compromise its financial performance together with a clear explanation of driver-based budgeting and the benefits it will bring and some credible and practical next steps.

- Identify the key players involved, categorize them as either decision maker or decision influencer. Then once you have done this, informally sound out attitudes to moving to driver-based budgeting and try to assess the level of support they might provide. Some will be enthusiastic supporters, others will be indifferent and a few may be averse to such a change. As long as your immediate manager is not in this last group and supports your initiative, all is not lost. Senior managers in the main operational areas of any organization understand exactly what is involved in resource planning before line item expenses can be generated and budgets submitted. These people are likely to be among your greatest supports. So cultivate them early and get them to work with you to develop scenarios of how driver-based planning and budgeting will benefit them. Generally, if those at the front-line express their support for new ways of working, everyone else in the business sits up and listens.

- Actively canvass support and use your supporters to influence those resistant to change. You may never win their hearts and souls, but if you can make a pact that they will give it a try, you will have neutralized their opposition. Once you taste success, they will never vocalize their initial opposition.

- Ultimately the final decision to implement a new way of planning and budgeting may rest with senior executives or the board. But this is only the end of the process. If you have worked hard at preparing your business case and building up support beforehand, the outcome should be a foregone conclusion. But if you have not already found some champions within senior management and the board, do not underestimate their ability to veto the project. Preparing an ROI and painting a compelling picture of the benefits that driver-based budgeting will mean for both the business as a whole, and for them in particular, will help win the day. It is the board's responsibility to provide investors and analysts with guidance on future earnings and anything that helps them avoid issuing profit warnings ought to receive their support.

- If it helps you to progress towards your final objective, be prepared to accept compromise. For instance, few organizations are likely to fund a full implementation without an initial pilot study. In fact a pilot study may be just what is needed to convince sceptics of the ease of implementing driver-based budgeting and the benefits it can bring.

Having been given the green light to formally constitute a project, you may find your role changes. It may be that you are the ideal person to take on the role of project manager. But when you read the next section, you might conclude that the project would have a better chance of success with someone else at the helm. If this is the case, graciously accept whatever future role is offered to you and fulfil it to the best of your ability. Everyone will recognize the important contribution you made in bringing about the change.

Identifying the project manager

Few projects are completed without hitches and it would be foolish to assume otherwise. Issues and setbacks come in many forms: deadlines may be missed, budgets can overrun, and certain people and departments may be uncommitted and uncooperative. Anticipating these and identifying contingency plans to address them are all part of the responsibility of the project manager, making the selection of this person pivotal to the overall success of the project. As we shall see later, this person needs a kaleidoscope of skills. Evidently, they need to know something about accounting and budgeting and should have some knowledge of IT and systems. They also need to have good communication and time management skills. But managing projects requires exceptional people management skills as the individual will need to negotiate with colleagues and external service providers and identify and resolve potential conflicts.

There are a number of obvious choices, the most obvious being the person who is currently responsible for the budgeting process or the individual who first proposed the initiative. However, these people may lack some of the key skills and abilities required to successfully manage such a project. Inside a smaller organization, it is the responsibility of the senior management team to identify the mix of skills and abilities that are called for and identify a suitable candidate. Inside a larger organization, senior management may wish to delegate this responsibility to a project steering group made up of a cross section of senior managers from across the business. One of these senior managers may fulfil the role of project champion taking responsibility for coaching and directing the project manager and generally driving the project forward.

Ultimately the selection of the project manager is likely to involve some trade-offs, balancing strengths in some skills and abilities against weaknesses in others. Fortunately, critical areas of weaknesses, such as a lack of detailed knowledge of IT, can be compensated for in the composition of the project team. This should be made up of individuals who have the knowledge needed to represent their business function and the authority to ensure that it successfully completes any tasks it undertakes for the project. As the adoption of driver-based budgeting will undoubtedly lead to more frequent forecasting and more flexible and dynamic staffing, it always pays to include a senior member of the human resources function in the project team. In certain organization, working towards more flexible staffing may need an extended period of consultation and negotiation and without the early involvement of HR, there may be a delay in realizing some of the business benefits to be had from implementing driver-based budgeting.

In certain situations, an organization may decide that either it does not have a person with the experience and skills needed to manage the project or that the ideal person cannot be spared from their daily responsibilities. This may lead them to retain a consulting organization and one of their staff will become responsible for managing the project. Having someone external involved in a senior role in the project may actually help bring about the required change in that they may be less prepared to compromise and will be less concerned with the commonly accepted constraints and practices of the organization. External consultants are often used to overcome internal resistance and inertia and using their services may oil the wheels of the implementation.

Getting started

Having identified a project manager and selected a multi-functional team, the formal part of the project can start.

1. Developing a shared understanding in the project team

   Not everyone in the team may understand the project's objectives or exactly how driver-based planning and budgeting differs from any other form of planning and budgeting. Therefore, spending some time in a classroom situation to ensure that team members thoroughly understand what is involved is time well-spent. Much of the materials needed to run a session such as this will have already been developed and little preparation will be needed. But having team members able to talk confidently and enthusiastically about driver-based budgeting will enable them to satisfy the curiosity of people across the business and address their concerns before they can grow into major issues. It may be a small step, but it will pay back tenfold.

2. Set out the terms of reference

The terms of reference or project charter establishes the project within the organization and bestows authority on the project manager. You should not confuse the terms of reference with the project plan, which will be covered later. It is a much less detailed document. Ideally it should:

- Set out the business need for driver-based budgeting.
- Identify the high-level objectives. This may mean documenting the current planning and budgeting process and painting a vision of what it may look like in the future. There are organizations that provide external benchmarking data on financial processes such as management reporting and budgeting. If the organization subscribes to such a service, it may be appropriate to refer the objectives to peer organizations (e.g. currently we are in the third quartile of our industry in terms of speed of budgeting and our aim is to be in the first quartile in next year's syndicated report). Other objectives might include reducing the cost of excess capacity and improving the accuracy of forecasts.
- List who is involved in the project and their roles and responsibilities.
- Give some broad expectations of timelines and funding requirements. These need not be very detailed at this stage.
- Set out how and when team members will report to the project manager – and how and when the project manager will report to senior management or the steering committee.

One of the frequent shortcomings of terms of reference and project charters is that project goals and deliverables are vague and there is inadequate description of how much the system will be used and what the quantifiable benefits are to the organization. Imprecise and narrowly defined specifications frequently lead to the users being dissatisfied and disappointed with the end product. It is therefore imperative that business users contribute to drafting the terms of reference and both senior management and the project steering group formally review and approve them. If they are not prepared to free up some time from their day-to-day responsibilities to do this, ultimately they only have themselves to blame! Developing the terms of reference with detailed deliverables is one of the most critical steps in any project and this should be impressed on everyone involved. But once completed, the project manager and their team have the authority to proceed. They are up and running.

3. Establish a communications channel

Budgeting is a process that involves many people inside an organization. For some it can be an abhorrent and stressful event that they come to dread. For these reasons, managers across the organization will want to be kept informed of progress especially in the lead up to using a driver-based budgeting methodology for the first time. Today this is best done by using an internal extranet, but if this channel is unavailable you can always resort to newsletters. In addition to keeping managers informed with regular project updates and successes, an extranet is also an ideal repository for internally produced white papers, worked spreadsheet examples of driver-based budgeting and other relevant materials. The more you educate and reassure your audience, the less resistant they will be to change.

Many organizations also have internal "blogs" where the project manager can be given a forum to issue regular bulletins and managers can post their comments and questions. But before rushing into this you need to be sure that postings will be regular, ideally telling readers exactly when new postings will be made, and that comments and questions are replied to promptly. Unless it is kept fresh, it will soon become devalued.

Developing the project plan

1. Choosing a pilot site

You may think a pilot study to be an unnecessary step and certainly there are successful projects that have ignored this stage and gone straight to a full implementation. However they are useful, especially if, despite your best efforts, there are still a number of sceptics inside the organization. Not only do pilots studies help demonstrate the benefits of driver-based budgeting, they also help create a groundswell of enthusiasm among users. After hearing about the project from colleagues involved in the pilot study, it is not unknown for departments and business units to clamour to be the next involved in the roll out. Pilot studies also help uncover potential problems and risks as well as identify best practices and tips that can make the full implementation quicker and easier.

Because of the importance of the pilot study, you need to select a department or business unit that offers the greatest business benefits and the lowest risk. When making your selection you may find the following list of criteria useful:

- Does the department have highly repetitious activities or processes?
- Can the department measure the volume of activities or transactions?
- Is the department characterized by a high level of variable cost?
- Does the department have the potential to deliver good returns and benefits?
- Is the department small enough to complete the pilot study within the desired time frame, but sufficiently complex to provide a learning experience for the project team?
- Are the department's staff and management enthusiastic and willing to take part in the project?

If the project team or steering group want a methodology to help select a pilot site, you can weigh the selection criteria to reflect their relative importance by allocating a total of one hundred points across those you have identified, and then score each department out of five to reflect how well it fulfils each criteria. Table 10.1 shows a worked example.

Taking the time to work through this methodology removes some of the emotion from the process in that it allows participants to systematically evaluate departments against each criterion in turn. Should senior

Table 10.1 Example of an evaluation grid for selecting a pilot site

Selection criteria	Importance weighting	Department 1		Department 2	
		Score 1–5	Total	Score 1–5	Total
Clear set of drivers	40	5	200	3	120
Large amount of controllable cost	20	4	80	2	40
Commitment of departmental manager	10	3	30	3	30
Manageable scope	10	3	30	3	30
Potential benefits	10	4	40	4	40
Skills	5	2	10	5	25
Motivation of staff	5	2	10	5	25
Total	100		400		310

management or the steering group wish to review your choice of pilot site, you also have a detailed evaluation from them to review. For instance in the example above, the manager and staff in Department 2 are very enthusiastic and motivated to become involved in the project. However the department lacks a clear set of drivers, which has been assessed as the most important selection criteria.

The same methodology can be used on a larger scale to determine the order for rolling out the full implementation, perhaps grouping departments into three bands, A, B and C depending on how well they match up to the criteria.

2. Developing the project plan

The project plan details the individual tasks involved in the project showing who is responsible for their delivery, what cost is involved and the timings including deadlines, interdependencies, resource availability and project milestones. It may take a number of iterations to develop the project plan as costs and timings get firmed up. Plus you should always remember to build in a number of formal reviews where the project team, the steering group and the senior management can assess progress to date, sign off on key milestones and review the activities and resource required for the next stage. Gantt charts and project management software come into play at this stage.

One of the common failings in project plans is the failure to fully reflect the resource commitment of individuals so their personal workload outgrows their capacity to complete their allotted tasks. Eventually something has to give and it usually means a setback in achieving a key milestone, as well as a certain amount of frustration and gnashing of teeth. The only way to overcome this is to fully document all the tasks and the amount of work involved and cross reference this to individuals and their availability. Having their superior commit to their availability at the planning stage will also help keep progress on track. The same thing can also happen later in a project at the critical stage of user acceptance. Due to everyday business pressures, people are not able to devote sufficient time to user testing in a simulated environment. This is the ultimate test of whether the implementation meets the business specification before "going live" and it pays to stress the importance of this stage and gain senior management's commitment to making their staff available.

3. Identifying and Managing Risk

It is always better to formally identify any risks involved in the project upfront and evaluate whether their likely probability and potential impact makes it worth developing contingency plans. The project manager is responsible for ensuring this is done, but where the organization has an internal audit team there are definite benefits to be had from calling on their experience and skills. They will have a diligent approach to risk assessment and will ensure objectivity and independence.

Unexpected events do happen. Project managers move companies; critical deadlines are not met and IT encounter unforeseen systems issues. Attention should be directed to risks that have a high probability and a high impact, such as overruns on key tasks and overspend on budgets. Many risks can be mitigated by building some slack into timings and provisioning in the project budget. But throughout the project, it is one of the key responsibilities of the project manager to monitor ongoing risk and decide whether or not to implement contingency plans. If the project is delayed there is always the safeguard of the existing budgeting system to fall back on. One of the key milestones in any project is the decision to decommission the legacy system and this is usually not done until after a period of parallel running. However, users are likely to be voice dissent at the idea of entering data into two separate budgeting systems, so the sooner the new system gets through acceptance testing and the old system is turned off, the happier everyone will be.

Execution

Having developed the project plan and secured funding, it is time to get down to the "doing" where all the tasks identified in the project plan are carried out. Many of these, such as implementing new software, integrating the chart of accounts and historic line item expenses from the general ledger system and providing training to those in the IT and finance departments who are going to build the planning and budgeting model are taken for granted and will not be covered here. We will focus on the particular issues of building a driver-based planning and budgeting system.

1. Briefing the business users

Before you can start an implementation, all department heads and cost centre managers need to be thoroughly briefed about the project and formally introduced to the concept of driver-based budgeting. Much of material that has already been developed, such as the business justification and simple worked examples can be reused here and it is always worthwhile providing your audience with materials to take away and read in detail later. You should also remember that this might be their first introduction to driver-based budgeting and that it needs to be more than a "tell" session. If the project is going to be as complete success, you really need to win their "hearts and minds", so it should be as much "sell" as "tell". One way of doing this is involving satisfied users from the pilot study as they will be credible references and are often enthused by their experience.

2. Identifying the rules and relationships

Although you may have decided to start with a pilot study in a carefully selected business unit or department, a driver-based model usually starts at the beginning of the value chain at the point of demand generation. This can be the size and growth of the external market, the organization's market share, and sales and marketing activities being undertaken to grow the business. Therefore even if your pilot study involves a single department, such as the logistics function in a manufacturing environment or the claims department in an insurance company, you will need to involve people from other parts of the business in defining the rules and relationships that make up a driver-based planning and budgeting model. In a simple business it may be possible to get all key cost centre managers to participate in one or more workshops, but in more complex organizations, this might be too unwieldy and the only option is to model the business in a series of stages, starting with sales and marketing, then moving on to operations and finally finishing with the support and shared services functions. In manufacturing, where a plant may need to be run continuously to be commercially viable, capacity rather than demand may be the starting point for a driver-based model. In these instances, asset utilization, yield and average selling price have the most impact on financial performance, and optimal capacity drives the resource requirements in most departments. On paper, this type of model looks slightly different to a demand- or market-driven model, but most experienced manager working in such a business have no difficultly in explaining and mapping the relationships and rules.

Workshop delegates should be briefed on the purpose of the session beforehand and asked to bring with them any spreadsheets they use for resource planning and modelling at budgeting time. What you want delegates to do is to explain the modelling they do to generate their line item expenses. You can do this by having each delegate to make a short presentation or work through their spreadsheets. Some of their modelling will be based on arithmetic formulas using reliable data. Some may be less rigorous and simply based on assumptions or rules of thumb. In certain instances, there may be a complete absence of rules and relationships where they might be expected. For the moment, avoid making any value judgements about what you find. This is a public forum and if anyone looses face, you will lose their commitment to the project and may compromise its ultimate success. Just ensure that what is presented is understood so that the project team can document it later.

After the delegates have explained their own modelling, the second part of this preliminary workshop should be devoted to identifying any rules that span departments. This is best achieved by following the same order as the value chain, typically starting with sales and marketing departments, then operational departments and finally support and shared services functions and simply having delegates develop a series of flow charts to show how rules and relationships flow across the organization. In many workshops this ends up as a series of pages of a flip chart stuck up around the room. Again ensure that it is not too much of a "spaghetti-gram" and that the project team can document it later. By the end of the workshop, delegates are usually motivated by their joint achievement and totally committed to the project, so it is worth investing the time to make this stage a success. For the majority, it will be the first time anyone in finance has ever had any discussion with them about planning!

There are other ways of identifying drivers, rules and relationships and these may be used to supplement a workshop. Any organization that already does ABC will have a detailed set of resource drivers and cost drivers as well as reliable data on driver volumes. Because this data already exists there may be a temptation to forego involving users in a workshop. However this may cause issues later. Many managers may only have a limited understanding of ABC and what it involves, so it is always better to give them the opportunity to review and ratify such data and how it might be used in planning and budgeting. Similarly any organization that uses scorecards may have a strategy or success map and although these usually only include high-level drivers, they should not be ignored when trying to understand and map the logic of the enterprise.

3. Document and review the rules and drivers

Immediately after the workshop, the rules, relationships and drivers should be documented. This should be done systematically and in a considerable amount of detail, as eventually it will become a working document for those who will be building the budgeting model.

Ultimately there are two categories of rules and it will be easier for the model builders to identify these separately:

- *Enterprise-wide rules*, such as pensions which are always a fixed percentage of salary regardless of department and which no one inside the organization other than the HR Director can amend.
- *Departmental rules*, which are owned by a cost centre manager who can alter the drivers each time they budget and re-forecast.

However, the workshop may have revealed different approaches to budgeting for other line item expenses such as Travel and Entertainment and Office Supplies. Ideally line items such as these, that are minor items in every department, should be budgeted for in a consistent manner.

At the same time, you need to decide the minimal amount below which there is little value in writing rules to make a line item driver based. For instance, small departments with a handful of staff and therefore very little expense in salaries may actually be carrying out activities that are driven by demand. However, it may take a large increase in the amount of demand to trigger the need for an additional member of staff. In such instances, it may be more expedient simply to have users enter salary expenses as they always have.

Documentation should include the following information:

- A name and index number for each rule.

  E.g. Staff planning rule in Claims department, CD2

- Details of the "owner" of the rule.

  E.g. Martin Payne, Claims Manager

- A detailed description of the rule, the demand driver, resource consumption rates and any "rules of thumb" that are used.

  E.g. Staff resources depend on the number of claims processed in a month. Currently 90% of claims classed as "straightforward" taking 12 minutes to process and 10% of claims are classed as "complex" requiring further information from the policyholder and detailed investigation. These take 40 minutes to process. All straightforward claims are processed in the month they are received while only 70% of complex claims are processed in the month they are received, the remainder being processed in the following month. As a rule of thumb, the Claims Manager uses a figure of 90% for theoretic capacity; the remaining 10% allowing for training, team meetings and unplanned absences. There is a Claims Supervisor for every team of ten Claims Agents.

- Details about the granularity of detail used for modelling; that is whether it varies by the core modelling dimensions of product, version or period.

  E.g. Although the department processes claims received from policy-holders who represent different levels of risk and who pay different premiums for different levels of cover none of this detail that is used elsewhere in the business, is used in this rule. It is simply the total number of claims received in a period.

- A worked example of how the rule is used for (a) forecasting and budgeting when only the total number of claims is a forecasted figure, (b) historic reporting when the actual number of straightforward and complex claims are known figures that can be taken from the claims management system. This should show whether the user will be able to manually override calculated figures in any part of their forecasting and budgeting.
- Details of how the drivers used in the rule are impacted by changes in other departments – and how this rule itself impacts demand in other departments.

  E.g. The key driver used in this rule (i.e. the volume of claims received) is a result of the number of live policies and the claims frequency. The rule itself determines the number of claims agents impacting recruitment, payroll and other activities in HR, desktop support in IT and space planning in Facilities.

- Details of how much data is involved each period and whether it is going to be imported from any databases or operational systems or simply manually entered.

  E.g. Accurate historic data on the number of straightforward and complex claims can be taken from the claims management system.

However as this is only two figures each period, this data will be manually entered by the Claims Manager on the second day of the following month as part of the data replenishment routine prior to month-end reporting. All staff details and salary expenses will be imported from the HR system and the general ledger at the same time.

- Outlines of what type of reports and screen views users feel they need. Making amendments to reporting screens is not an onerous task and they can be tailored to individual's needs as they start to work with the application. The most recent generation of packaged budgeting applications now allow users to define their own views of their data. But trying to get it halfway right from the outset always saves time later.

If each rule is documented in a consistent format and forms a separate document that is part of a larger "rule dictionary", it can be formally reviewed and "signed off" by its owner. While this is being done, the project team should investigate any anomalies identified during the workshop such as departments that currently do not use rules for certain line items although they are seemingly driver based so that resource requirements fluctuate with demand. Sometimes analysing historic data and comparing demand against the amount of resource available will result in new rules and relationships being identified and these will need documenting and including in the model. But at other times, it may be that the amount of resource and expense involved is too small to warrant inclusion.

4. Agree the planning and budgeting period to use

In discussing forecasting in Chapter 2, it was suggested that always looking forward 18 months is an appropriate planning period to use in that halfway through the current year there is always a complete forecast of the following year. To derive the real benefits of driver-based budgeting this should be the minimum period considered and the characteristics of business and the markets it operates in may suggest using a longer period. Likewise companies operating in dynamic markets such as express delivery and transportation or companies manufacturing perishable products such as fresh foods may wish to budget using weeks as period rather than months.

It is better to discuss these issues and reach an agreement before any work starts on building the budgeting model as any subsequent change will involve restructuring the model and rebuilding data entry screens and reports.

5. Agree the planning and budgeting cycle and map the processes involved

Many organizations implement more frequent forecasting and move away from a fixed annual budgeting cycle iteratively. They start out from their current practice of perhaps an annual planning budgeting cycle that kicks off at the beginning of September and a single mid-year re-forecast at the end of June and introduce the new approach without any changes to this calendar. This gives the users time to experience the new system and decide for themselves that driver-based budgeting makes everything quicker and easier. Then they might implement quarterly or monthly rolling re-forecasts and, once users are comfortable with that, abandon the annual budgeting cycle completely and implement quarterly strategic reviews.

There are a number of obvious benefits in adopting this iterative approach. It removes some of the politics that might arise from setting seemingly audacious goals at the outset and it allows cost centre managers the opportunity to discover for themselves that their life has really been made easier. The downside is that it can take a couple of years to achieve the desired endgame and get the maximum benefits. Some halfway house is the optimal timescale to aim for. The good news is that increasing the frequency of re-forecasting has little impact on the design of the budgeting model and little rework is needed to input screens and reports.

6. Documenting the planning and budgeting, and re-forecasting processes

The planning and budgeting, and re-forecasting processes also need to be considered at this stage. You may decide that these are identical. However, if you decide there is little to be gained from including certain cost centre managers in mid-year re-forecasts, you will end up with two distinct processes. Each needs mapping across two distinct dimensions:

*   First, the processes need to be mapped horizontally across the organization according to the flow of rules and relationships that were identified in the workshop. This determines the sequence in which individual cost centres will be called on to contribute to a budget or a re-forecast. In demand-led models this will broadly follow the flow of sales and marketing, operations and finally the support functions.

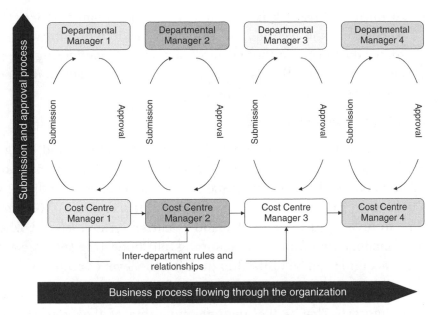

Figure 10.2   Horizontal and vertical processes in planning and budgeting

- Then the processes need to be mapped vertically, up and down the reporting lines of the organization, to reflect the budget submission and approval routine between the individual cost centre managers and their superiors. Figure 10.2 diagrammatically shows these relationships.
- In a complex organization, using a desktop process modelling package makes this task easier and quicker, providing "swim-lanes" that help track how the process flows across departments.
- In most organizations, users are only allowed to view their own data and that of their direct reports so that information of a sensitive nature, such as salaries, remains confidential. However there are always certain people inside the organization, such as members of the human resources and finance departments, who need access to data that others are routinely denied. As part of the mapping process above, the security access of individual users needs to be identified. This is not as onerous as it sounds as most software packages allow security and access rights to be assigned to groups of users and provide defaults and overrides. As the majority of users fall into one of the categories of cost centre manager, departmental manager or head of department, most of the work involves identifying and documenting the access and security rights of the exceptions.

- Again once this task is completed, it is important that everything is checked and verified by the users as it will form the main source document for those commissioned with configuring any work management tool that is going to be used to manage and expedite budgeting submissions and re-forecasts.

7. Refining forecasts of demand

The most critical input into any driver-based planning and budgeting model is the forecast of demand as this drives the volume of many of the other activities that drive resource requirements and expenditure right across the organization. Because of its importance, it is worth investing time to review exactly how demand is currently forecast and whether the functionality of any new planning and budgeting software that is being acquired can be utilized to improve the level of accuracy.

For many organizations the current forecast of demand is simply the sales forecast. That is the amount and value of the product sold or services provided. But for other organizations such as charities, social services and government departments, the forecast of demand might be the number of individuals rehoused, the number of grant applications received or inspections carried out. But the concept of demand does not make sense for some other organizations, such as armed forces and fire services, which provide "capability" that may or may not be called upon. But first let us discuss organizations that have sales forecasts and quantified forecasts of demand.

Web-based planning and budgeting applications that are based around multi-dimensional databases and have automatic consolidation routines make it easier to forecast at a greater level of detail and for more people to become involved in the process. But no one is going to go to the extreme of having every salesperson forecast every product line for every customer by each distribution channel for every period. Even with the best software, this would be too onerous. Somewhere in between lays a happy medium that reflects the Pareto rule where the important products and customers that account for 80% of the volume or revenue are forecast at a more detailed level and the rest are forecast at a higher level, perhaps using the functionality provided by the software to automatically spread this to a more granular level of stock-keeping unit according to the most recent trends.

Do not forget that rules can be used in modelling demand and revenues in exactly the same way they can be used to model resource requirements and line item expenses. Ultimately an organization's sales depend on the number of consumers in its market, the amount of product or service each one consumes and its share of that market. All this can be modelled, perhaps even linking back the number of consumers in the market to changes in demographics. Similarly it may be possible to generate greater accuracy in demand forecasts by forecasting repeat business from existing customers separately from business coming from new customers that need to be acquired in the future.

Many packaged budgeting solutions provide a battery of statistical forecasting functions that can account for factors such as underlying growth trends and seasonality and generate lines of best fit. While such functionality has limited use in forecasting line item expenses as simply extrapolating historic tends provides little insight into what is actually happening within an organization, it can help bring greater accuracy to forecasts of demand in the short to medium term. However, even this limited use of inbuilt forecasting functionality can lead to a blinkered view of the future. Resource plans and budgets need to be linked to the bigger picture of the overall market and economy. That means systematic tracking factors such as the size and growth of the various markets and market segments that an organization competes in together with a rigorous assessment of economic, demographic, competitive and technological factors that influence the evolution of the market in the longer term. The easiest way to achieve this is by developing a driver-based strategic planning model with a longer time horizon and integrating it with the annual or rolling driver-based resource planning and budgeting model. Many packaged budgeting applications enable models to be linked so that data from one can populate another so that a top–down strategic planning model can be directly linked to a bottom–up operational planning and budgeting model. Organizations that systematically monitor the bigger picture and can detect, assess and react to the early signs of change in their markets are always going to be more successful than those that have not provided themselves with these capabilities. Continually comparing the longer-term strategic view of the business with the short-term operating plan at periodic review meetings generates an informed debate that leads to better decisions being made.

But forecasting demand goes beyond a traditional sales forecast where the focus is only sales volumes and revenues. The resource requirements in a credit control department are driven by the number of active customers and the proportion that do not submit their payments within the prescribed terms of trade. Likewise the resource requirements in a fire station to meet a certain level of capability or "readiness", such as being able to dispatch a tender to 95% of call outs within 5 minutes, depends on factors such as the distribution of call outs over a typical week and the probability of call outs occurring simultaneously. If this type of demand data is not already being recorded, some data analysis and modelling will need to be done to establish a baseline against which to forecast as well as a process put in place to capture the data in the future. This is a relatively easy task for any organization that has a central data warehouse and business intelligence tools to query and report the necessary data. But where this is not the case, a certain amount of pragmatism is needed and this may mean going live with some very rough and ready estimates gained through sampling until more reliable data is available. But ultimately if department does not currently plan using demand volumes and resource consumption ratios, you should first ask whether there is sufficient amount of controllable cost to make adopting a driver-based approach worthwhile.

8. "Go-live" acceptance criteria

If all of the above steps are followed, those building the budgeting model should be able to make rapid progress without having to constantly stop and go back to the user community to find out how to incorporate unresolved issues. There is always project creep in one direction or another. Sometimes project deliverables are dropped from scope when it is discovered that they are slightly more difficult to achieve than was initially thought and are classified as non-critical to go live. At other times, project creep goes the other way and requirements grow beyond the initial specification requirement. Where this happens the steering group should sign off for the decision and the project manager should access what impact the enlarge scope has on timings and budgets, bringing into play any contingency plans when the need arises.

Throughout the project, members of the project team should diligently maintain an issues log and although many will be resolved as the project progresses, this should be totally cleaned down as a part of acceptance testing so that all critical issues have been resolved to the satisfaction of the users. If all the project deliverables have been assigned acceptance criteria, it is a relatively simple matter to document that the users are satisfied that they have been attained (perhaps with a few non-critical deliverables still outstanding), and have the project steering group make the decision to go-live.

9. Documentation

If you have followed the guidelines set out above and systematically documented the business requirement and the rules and relationships that underpin your budgeting model diligently, logging authorship and maintaining version control, you will make life easier for yourself in the future. There is a natural tendency to skimp on this important step, especially when it involves retaining external service providers to complete the task and incurring additional fees. But if the documentation is done thoroughly and stored securely in both electronic and hard copy formats, they will always be there for future reference. The most obvious users of this documentation are those who need to amend the budgeting model due to structural changes in the organization or simply the desire to add other functionality. Having a detailed set of cross-referenced documents to work from will greatly accelerate their work, saving both time and costs, which can be an important consideration. But there are numerous other external stakeholders who might wish to review the documentation. As we discussed earlier, there is increasing pressure and impending legislation for companies to provide guidance on future earning and a company's planning and budgeting system is fundamental to providing such guidance. So in the future external auditors may want to review the process and controls built into any planning and budgeting system and are likely to require documentation. The same goes for external certifiers assessing an organization's internal quality management for accreditation against standards such as the internationally recognized ISO 9000.

Post-project support

1. Maintaining the solution

As most budgeting packages use data entry and reporting screens that have the familiar look and feel of spreadsheets, users rarely require much in the way of training. Many users will have been involved specifying their part of the model, how it works and the reports they need and will quickly become familiar with working with the application. It may be necessary to hold some short briefing sessions for users, but in many instances instructions about how to use an application can be included in an e-mail together with a hyperlink to an appropriate landing page. Where a work management tool is being used to monitor and expedite the budget submission process, it can be configured to automatically send out personalised e-mails that lead individual users to their specific home page.

Of more concern is the availability of trained and knowledge staff able to maintain and amend the solution once it has gone live and the project team has been disbanded. There are many instances where solutions that met the needs of the business and totally delighted users have fallen into disuse because the business failed to provide the resource to maintain them. Ideally, finance specialists should be involved in helping specify and build the budgeting solution, working as part of the project team so there is adequate opportunity for knowledge transfer. Then once the solution is implemented, and right throughout its lifetime until it is finally decommissioned and replaced many years into the future, the organization should always ensure that it has an adequate number of people able to amend and enhance it. Talented finance staff who have software skills are a valuable resource and are always attractive to other employers, not least software vendors and consulting organizations. Because of this, organizations need to maintain skills matrices and always have a back-up position if a key member of staff leaves as the alternative is to constantly call on expensive external resources.

2. Post-project evaluation

The project manager and project team will do themselves a disservice if they only evaluate the success of the project at a single instance in time. Initially any driver-based planning and budgeting model will rely on estimates and best guesses for certain demand volumes and resource consumption rates and it will take a few rounds of budgeting and re-forecasting, where the variances between forecast and actual values become rapidly apparent, to refine its accuracy. Similarly, the users will need time to become familiar with the new process.

The criteria for success should have been set out in the terms of reference and investment appraisal and these should be periodically assessed over a number of months. If success is measured by reducing the cost of excess capacity to less than 4% of operating costs, monitor it and report on it. If success is defined as being able to forecast quicker, measure the improvement and communicate it across the organization. Someone will also ask about bankable cost savings and whether the project achieved its forecast return on investment, so rework the calculation and share the results. But do not ignore the users. Interviews or self-completion surveys will provide valuable feedback that will help to set the priorities for future enhancements.

Changing the role of finance

Implementing driver-based budgeting has the potential for changing the role of people in the finance team and it is always best of this is considered well before the implementation goes live. Any finance function in any organization has three broad roles:

- Processing transactions such as purchase orders, invoices and payments and recording these transactions in financial systems so that an auditable set of accounts can be produced.
- Ensuring that policies and controls are in place to prevent fraud and that generally accepted accounting principles are followed in line with the requirements of regulators.
- Providing information to the CEO and other managers so they can make decisions that help achieve strategic objectives and lead to a better financial performance in the future.

Of all these roles, the last undoubtedly has the most value to the organization and in recent years there has been a drive to re-engineer finance functions so they can spend more time dedicated to the area of strategy and decision support. The implementation of better financial systems and more automated processes should have enabled this to happen. However in recent years, there is little sign of any substantial shift on focus. In 2005, the findings of IBM Business Consulting's annual global CFO survey[1] showed that finance departments still spent 47% of their time on processing transactions. This represents a substantial reduction over 1999 when the figure stood at 65%, but little change from 2003, when the figure had already dropped to 50%. This shows that the transformation of the finance function has stalled and one might have suspected that this was due to the increased need to devote resource to ensuring compliance with a growing body of regulation. However, the majority of CFO's surveyed in the report were comfortable with the proportion of time being devoted to governance and stewardship and this suggests that the main challenge is to move resource in the finance function away from transaction processing towards analysis and decision support.

It may have reached a temporary impasse, but it will happen. Finance departments will continue to streamline transactional processing, centralizing and standardizing core financial processes, so that they can enjoy the step changes that shared services initiatives can deliver. Organizations will implement suites of fully integrated performance management applications that will provide better insight into both financial and operational performance and free management accountants from their over-reliance on labour-intensive spreadsheets. All this will change the role of finance and the skills and attitudes required to be a successful management accountant. The deskbound jobs of processing transactions and reporting are likely to end up in shared services units in some remote location where there is an adequate supply of trained staff and wage rates are low. The remaining role requires a different type of management accountant. This change was reported in research into the future of management accounting conducted by Professor Bob Scapens and colleagues published in 2003[2]. But in the short time since then, the emerging concept of corporate performance management where financial and non-financial data are united in methodologies such as driver-based planning and budgeting have gained credence providing a more structured context in which to explore what the future may hold for the management accountant.

No matter what the outcome is, the role is likely to transcend both words in the current job title. The traditional focus on "management" will be broadened upwards into supporting strategic decision making and downwards into supporting operational decision making. At the same time the focus on "accounting" will extend well beyond financial performance and embrace the non-financial drivers of value creation. At one level this wider remit of becoming the guardians of value creation means becoming involved in implementing a wider range of performance management methodologies spanning process improvement initiatives to reduce costs in operational areas to external benchmarking and industry analysis that underpin strategic decision making. If the business is to retain the role of management accountant in any shape or form, they will need to add value. Finance will be expected to understand customer, product and channel profitability, to have in place processes and metrics so that employees can report against actions that support corporate strategies and to provide managers with resources at short notice based on a rapid evaluation of how the decisions they take today are likely to impact financial performance in the future.

A number of factors are already impacting the role of the management accountant. First, many organizations have already a solid base of transaction processing and reporting which is liberating the management accountant from many of the laborious and time-consuming activities of the past. Second, the easier interconnectivity of software and the benefit of web-based applications is allowing organizations to improve their performance management capabilities. Planning and forecasting is being expanded to a broader group of users so that key non-financial business drivers that determine revenues and costs can be more frequently updated while being integrated with other previously stand-alone methodologies such as ABC. Finally, achieving a superior financial performance that results in the creation of shareholder value is increasingly dependant on having superior business analytics and performance management capabilities. Enterprises that effectively deploy driver-based budgeting and the other methodologies that go to make up corporate performance management are likely to outperform their competitors. The converse is also likely to be true; organizations that are not on the path to transforming their performance management capabilities are likely to underperform their peers, perhaps even fail. Management accounts who find themselves inside such organizations, where their role shows little sign of changing, have but three choices: put up and shut up, get out or pick up the gauntlet and take on the role of change agent within the finance function.

There is no telling exactly where the role of the management accountant may end up; the only safe prediction is that the responsibilities and job titles held by management accountants in the future will become much more varied than today. As organizations move away from the ubiquitous and labour intensive spreadsheet towards more specialist integrated applications, a growing proportion of management accountants will find themselves in a hybrid role between finance and IT as programme managers responsible for implementing and maintaining major performance management methodologies. Others will find a parallel role as the interface between finance and the main transactional systems deployed within the organization such as ERP, CRM and SCM.

But the most interesting role is that of working alongside decision makers at all levels of the business and providing them with insight and assessment to help them make better decisions that will improve financial performance in the future. This is already beginning to happen and some organizations have got to the stage that they now consider that the job title of management accountant does not reflect what their people do. In one company, the team have been retitled, "Performance Analysts" headed by a Director of Performance

Management, with each team member working as part of a business unit or department. Not everyone will make this transition. The new role requires people who combine sound accounting skills, a broad understanding of the business and the ability to develop an in-depth understanding of key business processes and commercial issues. Those that succeed and become valued members of the management team will be creative and offer line managers new ways of looking at things. Providing managers with information that shows that they overspent against their budget on a particular line item does not add value even if you could provide the report on the stroke of midnight on the last day of each month. Managers probably knew that was likely to happen at the start of the month when their workload rocketed and they had to recruit temporary staff. What they need is help in managing the future. This means gaining better visibility of future demand and greater agility in realigning resources to cope in the most cost effective way. All of this suggests that driver-based planning and budgeting is going to become one of the methodologies that will drive the change in the role of the management accountant. Any organization that implements driver-based planning and budgeting will find that its management accounting team are forced to get more deeply involved in the operational dimensions of the enterprise. Any organization that wants its management accountants to add value will find itself moving away from traditional budgeting and adopting a driver-based approach to planning and budgeting wherever it is feasible. It may be the ideal Trojan horse for any CFO looking to transform their finance team.

Summary

Implementing a solution to support driver-based planning and budgeting is undoubtedly more complex than implementing a traditional budgeting solution that only collects and consolidates individual contributor's submissions. It requires systematically identifying the rules and relationships that contributors already use in modelling their resource requirements and mapping them between business processes and departments. Many management accountants are daunted by this task and it can and does deter organizations from adopting a driver-based approach to budgeting. This is a pity because experience suggests that if the recommendations set out above are followed, the task can be completed quickly and helps build a bond between the users and the finance team. It also provides members of the finance function with a much deeper understanding of the operation than they might have previously had and help them prepare for the type of challenge that may be required of them in the future.

Notes

1 The Agile CFO, A study of 900 CFO's Worldwide, available at www.ibm.com.
2 The challenge of Management Accounting, Robert W. Scapens, J.E. Burns and Mahmoud Ezzamel, Elsevier/CIMA 2003.

Conclusion

Planning and budgeting is already one of the most important activities that an organization undertakes in the face of persistent uncertainty and investors wanting greater transparency into anticipated returns, its importance will increase until it becomes a frequent topic of boardroom discussion. It warrants this level of attention.

The current debate about budgeting focuses on hygiene factors. It takes too long; it costs too much and causes finance folk to rip out their hair. Automating the current budgeting process with software relieves much of the workload and frustration in the finance department but does little for the line manager and ultimately little for the organization as a whole. Typically it fails to enable more frequent re-forecasting or provide the organizational agility that is needed to compete in today's markets. Driver-based planning and budgeting, or predictive budgeting as it is sometimes called, provides an easy and low-risk way of transforming the traditional budgeting process so that the organization has better visibility into the future and can detect and respond to issues faster and more effectively.

The methodology is still in its infancy. Few planning and budgeting software packages can easily support driver-based budgeting and few organizations have comprehensively adopted it, although an increasing number have it on their roadmap. Research[1] carried out by global advisors, The Hackett Group, has already found that world-class companies who outperform their peers and do so with less volatility in their operating profits are more likely to have fully integrated operating planning and budgeting processes. Other global analysts suggest that driver-based budgeting or predictive budgeting will not become mainstream until the second decade of the century. So with some organizations already reaping the benefits, and others intent on adopting the approach in the near future, any organization that is setting out to adopt driver-based planning and budgeting is hardly in the vanguard. There is a growing body of expertise and experience to call upon. On the other hand, any organization that deliberates too long may well find that its planning and budgeting capabilities increasingly restrict its agility.

Note

1 *World Class Enterprise Performance Management*, The Hackett Group, 2006.

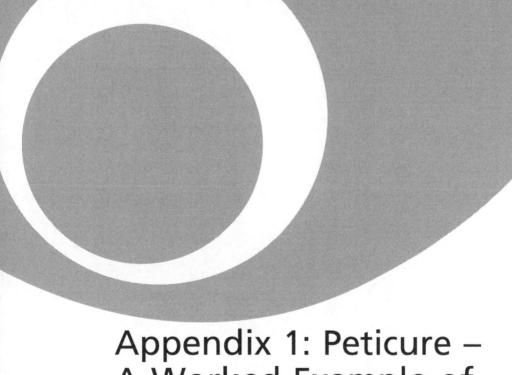

Appendix 1: Peticure –
A Worked Example of
Driver-Based Budgeting

This is a worked example of a driver-based budget for the claims department of Peticure, an insurance company that provides policies for cover for veterinary fees for companion animals. In other words, it is a healthcare for dogs and cats. Insurance is a sector that is well suited to driver-based budgeting, having lots of highly repetitive activities such as processing new business applications and paying claims.

Premium calculation

Being a consumer market with a large volume of customers all paying the same premium for the same policy, even the premium calculation can be done using drivers. Being a discretionary purchase, pet insurance is mainly purchased by households with higher levels of income, traditionally described as being social groupings ABC. Calculating the premium starts by gathering data on the number of such households from government statistics. Most of this data is only provided on an annual basis but year-on-year comparisons will give some idea of the annual growth rate and these can be used to provide an estimate for each month in the future year's budget (abbreviated to BY in Table A1.1). It is estimated that there will be 11.30 million such households in January and that this will have grown to 11.35 million by December.

Other syndicated market research also suggests that just over a third of these households own pets and that on average a pet-owning household will own 1.15 pets, that works out to roughly one household in five owning two pets. This research also suggests that just over 27% of pets are insured and that the percentage of pets with veterinary fee cover is steadily growing. Multiplying all these factors together gives the total estimated population of insured. In January of our budget year, this is estimated to be 1,285,982 rising to 1,300,134 by the end of the year. Syndicated market research also provides estimates of market share and this can be used to project the number of pets that Peticure insures. As management accountants increasingly find themselves freed from the drudgery of processing transactions and crunching numbers, they are going to have more time to work alongside business managers to help them make better decisions. If they are helping them to build a budget model such as we are doing here, they will soon encounter external sources of data, such as the syndicated survey we have referred to here. No one can doubt that external data is invaluable and in many situations it would be difficult to build a

Table A1.1 Driver-based approach for forecasting revenue and the volume of claims

All bold figs are calculated	Jan.	Feb.	Mar.	Apr.	May	Jun.	Jul.	Aug.	Sep.	Oct.	Nov.	Dec.
Market size and volumes												
# ABC1 households (millions)	11.30	11.31	11.31	11.32	11.32	11.33	11.33	11.34	11.34	11.35	11.35	11.36
% owning pets (%)	36.0	36.0	36.1	36.1	36.1	36.1	36.1	36.1	36.1	36.1	36.1	36.1
# pets per household	1.15	1.15	1.15	1.15	1.15	1.15	1.15	1.15	1.15	1.15	1.15	1.15
% insuring (%)	27.42	27.42	27.43	27.44	27.45	27.46	27.47	27.48	27.49	27.50	27.51	27.51
Total number of insured pets	**1,285,982**	**1,287,264**	**1,288,547**	**1,289,831**	**1,291,116**	**1,292,402**	**1,293,688**	**1,294,976**	**1,296,264**	**1,297,553**	**1,298,843**	**1,300,134**
Market share (%)	**31.1**	**31.5**	**31.9**	**32.2**	**32.6**	**33.0**	**33.3**	**33.6**	**34.0**	**34.4**	**34.8**	**35.1**
# Insured by peticure	**400,466**	**405,546**	**410,691**	**415,902**	**421,181**	**426,530**	**430,779**	**435,104**	**440,524**	**446,022**	**451,599**	**456,237**
Volumes by month												
# Insured pets at start of month	**395,448**	**400,466**	**405,546**	**410,691**	**415,902**	**421,181**	**426,530**	**430,779**	**435,104**	**440,524**	**446,022**	**451,599**
Cancellations during month (%)	0.100	0.100	0.100	0.100	0.100	0.100	0.100	0.100	0.100	0.100	0.100	0.100
# Existing insured pets at end of month	**395,053**	**400,065**	**405,141**	**410,281**	**415,486**	**420,760**	**426,103**	**430,349**	**434,669**	**440,084**	**445,576**	**451,147**
# New pets added during month	**5,413**	**5,481**	**5,550**	**5,622**	**5,695**	**5,770**	**4,676**	**4,755**	**5,856**	**5,938**	**6,023**	**5,090**
# Insured pets at end of month	**400,466**	**405,546**	**410,691**	**415,902**	**421,181**	**426,530**	**430,779**	**435,104**	**440,524**	**446,022**	**451,599**	**456,237**

Revenues

Average premium per pet (£)	11.66	11.66	11.66	11.66	11.66	11.66	11.66	11.66	11.66	11.66	11.66	11.66
Total written premiums (£)	4,671,035	4,730,293	4,790,303	4,851,084	4,912,657	4,975,041	5,024,611	5,075,049	5,138,274	5,202,399	5,267,449	5,321,549
Insurance premium tax (%)	4	4	4	4	4	4	4	4	4	4	4	4
Total premiums net of IPT (£)	4,484,193	4,541,081	4,598,691	4,657,041	4,716,151	4,776,039	4,823,626	4,872,047	4,932,743	4,994,304	5,056,751	5,108,687

Claims

% of insured pets claiming	5.00	5.01	5.01	5.01	5.01	5.02	5.02	5.02	5.02	5.03	5.03	5.03
% claims paid	98.80	98.80	98.80	98.80	98.80	98.80	98.80	98.80	98.80	98.80	98.80	98.80
# claims	19,535	19,793	20,054	20,319	20,587	20,858	21,134	21,355	21,580	21,860	22,144	22,432
Amount of average claim (£)	152.37	153.89	155.43	156.99	158.55	160.14	161.74	163.36	164.99	166.64	168.31	169.99
Total claims (£)	2,976,534	3,045,967	3,117,013	3,189,716	3,264,122	3,340,276	3,418,229	3,488,553	3,560,587	3,642,815	3,727,023	3,813,266
Simple loss ratio (%)	66.38	67.08	67.78	68.49	69.21	69.94	70.86	71.60	72.18	72.94	73.70	74.64

driver-based budgeting model without knowing something about market size, market growth and market share. However, caution is needed when working with external data and it should be validated both against other external data and against any internal data. Ensure that it is consistent and if it is not, be prepared to make some adjustments until it reconciles. In this example the prevalence of pet insurance is not an audited figure. It is a finding from a market research survey. It was probably gained from asking a sample of adults whether they own pets, then asking those that do whether they insure them or not. This is actually a leading question; a negative answer perhaps reflecting a lack of concern and care for their cat or dog. Consequently any market research about pet insurance always has to be treated with caution. Reconciling the findings from market research with the number of pets that Peticure actually insures may lead to the conclusion that the market research overstates the actual figure. If that is the case, the amended figure should be used in any model.

Having arrived at the figure for the number of active policies during any month, this could simply be multiplied by the average monthly premium to give a revenue figure. However this is too simplistic for most purposes and in the example we have used an opening balance and closing balance for each month; the difference between the number of policies that have been cancelled during the month and the number of new policies added during the month. In the worksheet you will see that a monthly cancellation rate of 0.100% has been used and this would be a key driver in the budgeting model and something that would also be closely monitored in a balanced scorecard as any deterioration quickly reduces future revenues. Likewise if the number of new policies added during the month falls below the number of policies that are cancelled during the month, then the whole business starts to go into decline. Anyone working in a commercial role in this business would monitor these numbers closely; perhaps even more than the revenue number itself.

All that is needed to finish modelling the premium is to factor in the average monthly premium and to keep the model simple, all policyholders pay the same monthly premium for the entire year. In reality, policyholders are renewing their policies on a monthly basis and paying different premiums when they renew. But to reflect this we would need to build a more complex model with both a mid-term cancellation rate and an annual renewal rate. All that is left is to deduct the 4% insurance premium tax from the gross premium to give the net premium which totals £57.56 million for the budget year.

Cost of claims

Drivers are also used for calculating the cost of claims, the part of the model that would be the responsibility of the actuarial department. Typically actuaries would use their own expert models for analysis and forecasting, and all that is being shown in this budgeting model are figures for the frequency of claims (starting at 5% of all active policies in January and steadily increasing to 5.03% by December), the proportion of claims that are valid and are subsequently paid (98.8% throughout the year) and the average amount paid out for each claim. This is something that increases steadily throughout the year with the growing sophistication and cost of treatments and medications. Health insurers and pet insurers alike call it "claims inflation". Once the cost of claims has been calculated, it is possible to calculate a "simple loss ratio", a ratio of the cost of claims against net premiums. Again all of the drivers used in this budgeting model so far are KPIs and any insurer would monitor them continuously. They are that important. Now they are incorporated into a driver-based budget, any changes made to a driver in any future period or periods will automatically impact financial performance.

Claims handling

To complete this simple worked example, modelling has been extended to the staffing requirements, salary expenses and pension costs in the claims processing department. There is a Claims Manager and a Claims Supervisor and their salaries are provided, as is the average monthly salary of a Claims Agent. The staffing requirement has to be calculated by combining the forecast of the number of claims that has already been generated with some rules of thumb and relationships that the Claims Manager has observed and monitored ever since he took over the department. These are as follows:

- Of the claims paid that arrive in a month, 80% are simple claims and take 10 minutes to process. Of these simple claims, 90% are processed in the month they arrive, the rest in the following month.
- The remaining 20% of claims paid are complex claims and require investigation. They take 30 minutes to process. Of these complex claims, 50% are processed in the month they arrive, the other 50% in the following month.
- Assume that a normal working day is 7.5 hours and that with time for training, holidays and illnesses, only 90% of a Claims Agents' time is spent processing claims.

Knowing these simple relationships, it is possible to complete the staffing budget. But what if none of these relationships were known and the Claims Manager had previously prepared his annual budget by taking the previous year's salary costs and increased them in line with the actuarial departments forecast number of claims? Well if nothing changes during the year, with the ratio of simple claims to complex claims remaining constant and processing times constant, the forecast salary costs might not be too far removed from what has been calculated in this driver-based model. But should anything change, such as the company adopting a more rigorous policy to paying claims so that the percentage of claims paid falls from 98.8 to 95.0%, and automation speeding up processing so that it only takes 8 minutes to process a simple claim and our Claims Manager will have to resort to guesswork. Whereas with a driver-based budgeting model, he could feed in the new assumptions and quickly generate a new forecast for the department's expenses (Table A1.2).

Table A1.2 Driver-based approach to generating salary expenses in the claims department

All bold figs are calculated	Jan.	Feb.	Mar.	Apr.	May	Jun.	Jul.	Aug.	Sep.	Oct.	Nov.	Dec.	Total
Working days in the month	20	21	22	20	20	20	20	19	20	21	22	17	242
Total # claims	19,535	19,793	20,054	20,319	20,587	20,858	21,134	21,355	21,580	21,860	22,144	22,432	251,651
% Simple	80.00	80.00	80.00	80.00	80.00	80.00	80.00	80.00	80.00	80.00	80.00	80.00	
# Simple	15,628	15,834	16,043	16,255	16,469	16,687	16,907	17,084	17,264	17,488	17,715	17,946	201,321
# Complex	3,907	3,959	4,011	4,064	4,117	4,172	4,227	4,271	4,316	4,372	4,429	4,486	50,330
% Simple current month	90	90	90	90	90	90	90	90	90	90	90	90	
% Complex current month	50	50	50	50	50	50	50	50	50	50	50	50	
# Simple claims in current month	15,621	15,814	16,022	16,234	16,448	16,665	16,885	17,066	17,246	17,466	17,692	17,923	201,082
Time simple	10	10	10	10	10	10	10	10	10	10	10	10	
# Complex claims in current month	3,899	3,933	3,985	4,037	4,091	4,145	4,199	4,249	4,294	4,344	4,400	4,458	50,032
Time Complex	30	30	30	30	30	30	30	30	30	30	30	30	-
Total hours required to process claims	4,553	4,602	4,663	4,724	4,787	4,850	4,914	4,969	5,021	5,083	5,149	5,216	58,530
% Productive time	90	90	90	90	90	90	90	90	90	90	90	90	
Total work hours required	5,059	5,113	5,181	5,249	5,318	5,389	5,460	5,521	5,579	5,648	5,721	5,795	65,033

(continued)

Table A1.2 *(Continued)*

All bold figs are calculated	Jan.	Feb.	Mar.	Apr.	May	Jun.	Jul.	Aug.	Sep.	Oct.	Nov.	Dec.	Total
Hours per FTE in month	**150**	**158**	**165**	**150**	**150**	**150**	**150**	**143**	**150**	**158**	**165**	**128**	
FTEs required	**34**	**32**	**31**	**35**	**35**	**36**	**36**	**39**	**37**	**36**	**35**	**45**	
Salaries – Claims Manager (£)	3,000	3,000	3,000	3,000	3,000	3,000	3,000	3,000	3,000	3,000	3,000	3,000	36,000
Salaries – Claims Supervisor 1 (£)	2,042	2,042	2,042	2,042	2,042	2,042	2,042	2,042	2,042	2,042	2,042	2,042	24,500
Average Salary Claims Agent (£)	1,563	1,563	1,563	1,563	1,563	1,563	1,563	1,563	1,563	1,563	1,563	1,563	18,750
Salaries – Claims Agents (£)	53,125	50,000	48,438	54,688	54,688	56,250	56,250	60,938	57,813	56,250	54,688	70,313	673,438
Salaries – Total (£)	**58,167**	**55,042**	**53,479**	**59,729**	**59,729**	**61,292**	**61,292**	**65,979**	**62,854**	**61,292**	**59,729**	**75,354**	**733,938**
Pension (£)	**2,908**	**2,752**	**2,674**	**2,986**	**2,986**	**3,065**	**3,065**	**3,299**	**3,143**	**3,065**	**2,986**	**3,768**	**36,697**

Appendix 2:
Activity-Based Costing

Having survived the hype of the last two decades and proven its value many times over, activity-based costing (ABC) is back on the corporate agenda. After the initial burst of enthusiasm it enjoyed in the early 1990s, ABC came to be viewed as too time-consuming and laborious to be worth implementing. Collecting data that is not stored in any software system, such as the proportion of time a department's staff spend on various activities, can be particularly tedious so that models were recalculated infrequently and reports were quickly out of date and ignored by line managers. The ABC movement lost momentum as this negative perception spread. But having invested millions in new transaction systems and data warehouses and still found they do not know which customers and products are profitable or how much business processes cost, ABC is climbing the corporate agenda and is being adopted as one of the core elements of corporate performance management. The old guard, who have stood by it for decades, seem to have been proven right.

Companies that have done ABC well have realized benefits that make the initiative worthwhile. Research by David Southiere,[1] an associate partner with global consultants Accenture, suggests that an ABC project's identification of opportunities to remove non-value-adding activities can lead to step changes in the cost base of between 3 and 5%. His research also shows that ABC's ability to focus organizations on margin management and on growing profitable areas of business can lead to revenue growth in the range of 5–15%. After a decade of cutting direct costs in business units, IT shared services functions are coming under pressure to better control and understand their costs so that cross charging can be made more transparent and reflect actual usage. As roughly 50% of all the services provided by IT are truly "shared", ABC can help better understand what activities and resources are consumed by the services IT provides and it is being implemented by large IT shared services units where annual expense budgets typically run to eight-, and sometimes, nine-digit amounts. Realizing a 3–5% cost reduction on this type of spend soon pays for a modest ABC implementation!

It is variously estimated that 20–50% of the Global 1000 have implemented some form of ABC somewhere in their business and this is expected to grow in the coming years. The growing list of success stories is not the only reason that increasing numbers of organizations are investing in ABC. Another reason is that ABC projects tend to be more pragmatic than they were in the past when over-zealous management accountants and their retained consultants mindlessly followed textbook methodology and systematically decomposed the general ledger through hundreds and sometimes thousands of increasingly insignificant activities. Little wonder ABC got a bad name. Today's initiatives focus providing business managers with the right type of information that will help them make better decisions. Typically this means focusing on a smaller number of higher-level activities and providing more frequent reports so that the costs and profitability of things such as products and customers can be tracked over time.

A third factor in the renewed interest in ABC is the advent of web-based applications that eliminate much of the tedium and cost involved in collecting and collating data that cannot be downloaded from a software system. These newer applications allow users to refresh data in their models more frequently, and they enable managers to access reports from their desktop, then drill down into the data to better understand costs and profitability in their particular area of responsibility. Gone are the days of having to tailor endless reports for every department.

Finally, ABC is gaining some new attention because one of its founding fathers, Professor Robert Kaplan, has revisited it and renamed what the older exponents used to call derived drivers as "time-driven ABC". Kaplan sees time-driven ABC as an option for overcoming some of the downsides of traditional ABC. Proponents of time-driven ABC suggest that it removes the need for time-consuming and costly surveys, and that it is more accurate than traditional ABC. Both of these claims are debatable, but at minimum, time-driven ABC provides one more alternative for diverse companies looking to maximize the benefits of an ABC initiative.

Fundamentals of time-driven ABC

Typically in ABC programmes, activity costs are assigned to cost objects using an activity driver such as the number of times the activity is performed. Suppose, for example, that a particular department within an organization performs two activities: processing applications and chasing late payments. As Figure A2.1 shows, a manager who knows how staff spend their time and how they use the resources available to them can calculate the unit costs of processing an application and of chasing a late payment. This is done by simply assigning the costs to each activity according to what percentage of the department's time is spent on each activity.

Time-driven ABC adds another input to the costing equation: the cycle time for each activity. In this example it means the time required to process an application or to chase a late payment. When a company approaches the calculation

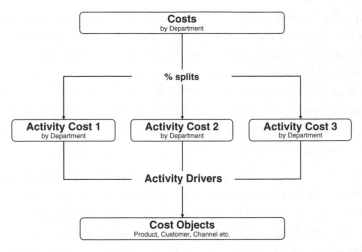

Figure A2.1 Activity-based costing "Time Splits"

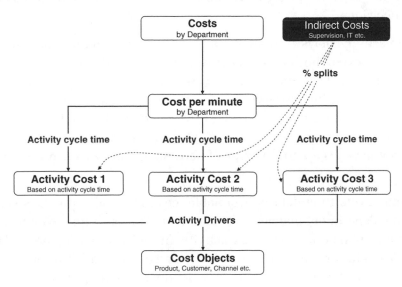

Figure A2.2 Time-driven activity-based costing

of activity-based costs with robust data on each activity's cycle time obtained from a transaction or processing system, it may be able to determine costs more accurately. Figure A2.2 shows the difference.

Time-driven ABC starts with the same information about departmental costs, but first calculates a cost per minute of resource and then assigns a cost to each activity depending on much resource time it has taken during the period. This is the multiple of the cycle time and the number of times the activity occurred. Because few managers are willing to reveal that their employees have much idle time, ABC using time splits rarely reveals excess capacity. This may not be an issue for organizations in which the purpose of the ABC initiative is to analyse current costs and profitability, but it is a problem for those that want to determine the optimal costs and profitability they could achieve if they eliminated all excess capacity.

A time-driven costing process automatically reveals any differences between the total time needed to carry out all of the activities performed by a department and the total amount of time the department's employees have available. This makes time-driven ABC a more rigorous methodology for ABC programmes in which better capacity management is an objective. Most retail banks use standard cycle times to determine the cost of certain activities in their branch network, the objective being to account for excess capacity in all costing and pricing decisions.

Still, subjectivity plays into almost all activity-cost calculations. Some functions do have cycle times that are easily and reliably retrieved from technology systems; automated call-handling software, for example, may be able to provide the manager of a customer service centre with exact figures on the department's average call duration during a certain time period. But such data cannot be generated for all corporate activities. Kaplan himself suggests that in functions that do not have access to this type of hard data, managers can estimate cycle times.

Even when cycle time data is irrefutable, costing usually involves subjective input from department managers. Time-driven ABC is simple to deploy only in a department that performs a single activity. In such a scenario, the total costs of the direct and indirect resources can be divided by the available resource to give a cost per unit of resource. However, most departments perform two or more activities that consume direct and indirect resources in different proportions, so some form of survey is required.

Consider the department in Figure A2.2. Although transaction systems may provide reliable cycle times and volumes for each of its employees' three activities, the manager must be involved in determining how the indirect costs are split and this is likely to involve simple percentage splits. There might also be a need to apportion some direct costs if different employees – at different salary levels – divided their time differently between the two activities.

If the salary level of employees involved in chasing late payments were considerably higher than that of employees involved in processing applications, this would need to be reflected in the calculation; multiplying the entire department's costs by the "time split" figures would not provide accurate cost results.

Proponents of time-driven ABC suggest that it leads to greater accuracy. As yet, there is no empirical evidence to prove this claim and the claim is difficult to reconcile with the suggestion that time-driven ABC can (and in many cases must) use estimates of cycle times. In the article "Time-Driven Activity-Based Costing" in the November 2004 issue of the Harvard Business Review, Kaplan and Steven Anderson write that "as a rule of thumb, you could simply assume that practical full capacity [of the workforce] is 80 percent to 85 percent of theoretical full capacity". Such an assumption calls into question the accuracy of the costing process's results.

Estimates and assumptions about key cost drivers are problematic for anyone using ABC, but they are of particular concern for public companies that use the methodology to assign costs to business units, subsidiaries and joint ventures in which profits are shared with another public company (for instance, publicly traded airlines' profit sharing on select routes). In the era of Sarbanes–Oxley, this means that an increasing number of ABC models are being audited and that any assignments which are either based on estimates or rarely updated may come under severe scrutiny.

To deliver an acceptable level of accuracy, time-driven ABC depends on robust and reliable data as much as any other methodology does. If the data comes from systems such as automated call-handling software and is regularly updated, then results will be accurate. However, if the information is out of date, or if it is based on estimates, the resulting cost information may include substantial errors. The difference between an estimate of four minutes and an estimate of four minutes eight seconds as the time required to handle an inbound telemarketing sales call may not seem large, but factored over 100 000 calls, it soon becomes significant.

Therefore, to be accurate, time-driven ABC requires as much data collection as traditional ABC. Each time a model is refreshed and recalculated, the duration drivers should be updated. Even the most repetitive processes change. Call-centre agents, for example, are frequently provided with new scripts in attempts to up-sell and cross-sell other products and services; such changes impact the length of each call. Collecting and collating data on cycle times means either regularly extracting the information from a transaction system or asking process owners to provide routine updates. Web-based ABC applications make such updates easy, and process management tools can expedite data collection.

Keeping the costing model up to date is difficult only when duration drivers are hard-coded into the software so that updates require IT intervention. This is important when shopping for software to support ABC: There is no valid reason for hard-coding cost drivers such as cycle times into the system, so look for applications in which updating all drivers is easy for the end user.

Although the label "time-driven ABC" has come into use only recently, many would argue that the approach is not new. There are numerous instances in which ABC models use activity cycle times and transaction volumes to calculate costs. Lever Fabergé, the home- and personal-care division of multinational consumer goods giant Unilever, has incorporated time-driven calculations alongside more traditional ABC methodologies since 1997. Unable to reliably assign resource costs to activities such as shrink-wrapping pallets in its distribution centres, Lever Fabergé decided to calculate the cost of the activity by measuring the amount of time involved and multiplying that by the unit cost of warehouse staff.

If asked, most ABC practitioners using such an approach would likely say they were using a "derived driver"; in other words, that they were combining two or more drivers (such as cycle time and transaction volume) to produce a third, derived driver, which they then used in assigning an activity cost to cost objects. It is also important to note that "traditional ABC" and "time-driven ABC" are not mutually exclusive. An ABC model does not have to use just one of these methodologies. In fact, time-driven ABC is not an appropriate methodology for all situations. In any organization, some functions – such as marketing, legal, research and areas of IT – include activities that are far from homogeneous and repetitive. Trying to force a time-driven methodology onto activities in which cycle times vary wildly is inappropriate; for those activities, an alternative methodology should be used.

For that reason, most ABC models are likely to be hybrids, using a time-driven approach or derived drivers where those calculations work best and using the more traditional methodology elsewhere. Organizations intending to implement ABC should ensure that the software they select is flexible enough to accommodate all the various cost drivers that are appropriate for all their various divisions. As companies realize how the different ABC methods can fit comfortably side by side in today's diverse organizations and as software vendors rise to the occasion and produce software that supports both forms of the methodology – interest in ABC will inevitably continue to grow.

Note

1 *The CFO Project*, CFO Publications, 2003.

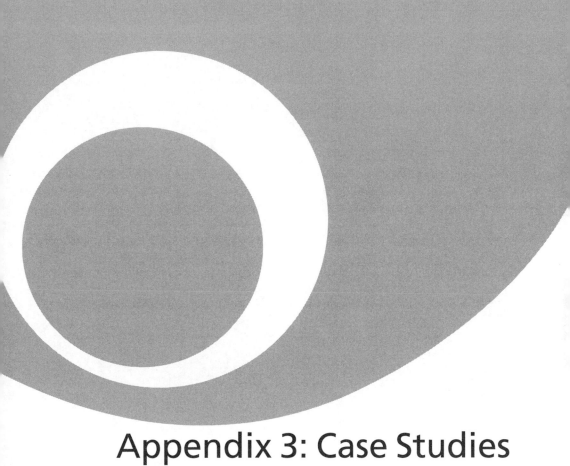

Appendix 3: Case Studies

TNT Express UK

TNT was formed following a merger between the Dutch postal service, PTT Post; and the commercial courier, TNT. The Group along with DHL, FedEx and UPS is one of the key players in global express delivery services in over 200 countries, owning its own operations in 62 of these with over 150 000 employees worldwide. TNT Express has always been sensitive to the downturns in the world's main economies and at the start of the new millennium, volume growth slowed. Fortunately some of the Express business in the larger economies such as the UK and France had the benefit of activity-based costing to assist with yield and cost management helping the divisions deliver exceptional results in 2002. This prompted Peter Bakker, CEO of TPG, to comment in the annual report "In summary, despite slower growth in volumes, Express performance was excellent. The fastest and most reliable approach grew EBITA by 51.5%, boosting margins for 4.0% in 2001 to 5.8% in 2002. Compliments to all the people in the Express division are well deserved."

However, while TNT Express had gained considerable benefit from implementing sophisticated cost and profitability analytics, their planning and budgeting was not in such good shape. What follows is an interview with Paul Witham, the financial strategy manager for TNT Express in the U.K.

Q: *TNT express is a business that truly spans the world, providing global shipping logistics and supply chain solutions. But what did TNT express do when it wanted to deliver a better budgeting process? Could you walk through the issues that made you rethink your budget process?*

Paul Witham: Well first we had significant budget growth, which was causing us some problems in trying to keep up with the pace of the business. On average, over the last 10–12 years the business has grown at 10% per annum. We'd also integrated over recent years as well with the international arm of our business. Part of that was the scale of the business and the size and growth of the business that we were experiencing and also the fast change in the business environment, with changes in competition, it's fast emerging that there are a small number of global players that are all fighting for a share of the market at the moment and so were experiencing quite a bit of competitive pressure as well. The biggest problem we have within the business is that we operate a shared user network and what we're constantly trying to do is balance the provision of resource or the provision of network for our business with the actual demand for our business, so it makes it very difficult and that is one the key things that we make an adequate return on our capital, to make sure that we have a successful growth.

Q: *What solution have you been using so far?*

Paul Witham: Obviously we've been trying to put this all together within spreadsheets. Spreadsheets are very fine tools but they have limitations, and what we're finding with that is that the budget process was taking longer each year. We actually finished in the third week of January last year for the budget because it was taking so long to get all these spreadsheets together and consolidate them and upload them into general ledger system. There are also other problems associated with spreadsheets, such as security and version control. We were getting different versions of the same budget, which was causing confusion and as a result of that we had a lot of people involved in the budget process, and it wasn't always constructive time that they were spending doing that process.

Q: *What goals were you looking to reach with a new solution?*

Paul Witham: The first thing we recognized was that we needed to replace spreadsheets within the budget process and obviously because of all those particular issues, one thing that we thought we would want to do as well would be to deploy this particular replacement over the web and because of the ease of deployment and the benefits it holds for a company of our size and the number of locations that we have. We also felt that we wanted to improve the version control by having a single version of the truth, a single database and basically we wanted to establish a platform for developing the budget process in its whole thing with integrating with strategy and integrating with the work we have done with activity-based costing. So it was very important to us that the product that we chose would enable us to do that even though we recognized in the early stages we would probably only be able to replace spreadsheets and get the benefits from replacing them.

Q: *And what tools did you chose to accomplish these goals?*

Paul Witham: We looked at a number of different products. We had done a prototype model earlier in the previous year with the tool, which basically just looked at one depot in isolation. We created a budget model within that which in the first stage did replace the spreadsheet process but then developed a more advance stage two prototype. We are also involved as well with our express division, which is based in Amsterdam, who were basically looking at all the tools that were available and around on the market at the time, and they went through a process of evaluating all those as well. So it served quite a useful purpose in getting the feedback and getting an input into what those other tools did compared to the one we looked at.

Q: *Paul, why did you choose the particular budgeting software?*

Paul Witham: From what we'd seen of the prototype, it was quite cutting edge, because it was a new product it was not trying to develop any old methods of doing things, and it was quite radical in its design. We recognized that and for one of the key things there was its ability to deploy the product easily, so that certainly attracted us to the product. We had done quite a lot of work with this company previously using another product for activity-based costing and in longer term we had identified there was that if we could get all the benefits of having an integrated activity-based costing/activity-based management system with the forecasting and planning software, there would be a lot more advantages to be had with having the two products together.

Q: *Now how has this solution transformed the budgeting process so far?*

Paul Witham: In terms of deployment, it's been very, very quick, and we basically started the project and got it through to a position where we were ready to go in eight weeks, which is very quick and a lot of that has got to be down to the ease of implementation with a product of this nature. What has happened is there has been a number of spin off benefits, mainly at the centre, where we were spending an awful lot of time trying to pull all these consolidations together. The process itself first of all gets a 'first hit' if you like from the depots, the first iteration of the budget. What we do with that information then is take it and use it as a basis for a lot of the central allocated costs. Where this process has helped us this time is that we've been able to turn that round very quickly where as previously we would have probably needed a week to work on some of the specific allocations had been turned around in maybe half a day. So it has enabled us to turn that process and speed it up to a great extent and put that information back to the depots so they can see a quicker, final view of their budgets.

Q: *You mentioned a quicker, final view, what other benefits have you seen?*

Paul Witham: There is obviously a great deal more control with using a single application. That's not just version control, that's security, and making sure that the whole group adheres to tighter timescales. The problem we had previously with spreadsheets was that they were attached to an e-mail system so it was a lot more difficult to try and control whereas, from the centre here we have got a perfect view of everything that's going on so we can control that a lot better. Where we were getting issues within the depots from a business point of view was how do they compile their budget? We were basically able to log on at the centre and look at the same sorts of issues, so that the dialogue was a lot easier. As a result of that, resolved a lot quicker. Basically end-to-end processes are a lot shorter. We certainly had a number of teething problems in the beginning because it was changed and people can be very often resistant to change. But the process itself has basically been cut in half and certainly towards the back end of the process it has become a lot easier and involved a lot less central time in preparing and populating our financial system with the final budget.

Q: *Now you said that phase one was already in place and yielding noticeable results, so is phase two in the process of being implemented?*

Paul Witham: Phase two, we are able to start now from January up until when we begin next year's budget process, which will start around August time. We have the opportunity to quite radically change what we are putting out there as budget application. Previously with spreadsheets we were asking depots managers to do was to create a financial statement – their P&L for a 52-week year focusing on revenues, costs and profits. Now no disrespect to the depot managers, but these are not always the terms that they use. They talk in more operational terms and what we want to do is make the budget process geared a lot more around that business planning aspect. So the managers themselves will have an understanding of what demand is going to be placed on them for a period of time. Now ultimately we have not talked about timescales yet, but currently we only prepare an annual budget because that has been the process that we've used. But what we want to do in stage two is start looking at the capability of doing more regular forecasts and updates. Over the last 2 or 3 years we have been working on an activity-based costing which has been predominantly used for customer profitability reporting. But obviously with the composition of that model what we are also able to identify is the combination or the relationship between the demands for services at our depots and the resource that we need to provide to deliver that high level of service. Because of the structure of the planning and budgeting model, it actually integrates seamlessly. The dimensionality in the model has the resource drivers and the activity driver elements which we can take from our previous work within activity-based costing to help identify what the total level of demand is placed on our depots and an efficient level of resource that we need to provide to deliver that high level of service. So that was another reason that we were quite excited and quite keen on taking the planning and budgeting product because of that functionality within there. And, from that point of view when we speak to a depot manager, what we would like to be able to construct the new budget process around is him talking about his own business and talking about the demands that are placed on him for the number of collections and deliveries he needs to do, the type of customers that he has, the profile of the freight that he moves, and from that we can take that sort of information and build the budget up from there. Then I think it will give a lot more benefit to the quality of the budget process that we are going through.

Fortis Health

Fortis Health has been in business since 1892 and is leader in the individual medical, small group, short term and student health insurance markets in North America. The company provides medical insurance to more than 1 million people in the United States. Its products are underwritten and issued by Fortis Insurance Company, John Aiden Life Insurance Company and Fortis Benefits Insurance Company. Fortis Health is headquartered in Milwaukee, Wisconsin, and has operations in Minnesota, Florida, Idaho and Ohio. Until 2004, when this case study was developed, Fortis Health was part of the Fortis Inc., a US-based financial services company that through its operating companies and affiliates had built leadership positions in a number of speciality insurance markets. Fortis Inc. in turn was part of Fortis, the European-based financial services provider active in the fields of insurance, banking and investment, which at the time ranked 31st in the Global 5000 based on asset value. Since then Fortis Health has been successfully divested by Fortis and now trades under the name of Assurant.

As Director of Performance Management, at that time Cathy Jorgensen recognized the importance of aligning decision making with corporate strategy. She also saw the immense benefit that could be received from more frequent budgeting and re-forecasting to reflect changes in the market. Existing budgeting practices at Fortis Health created challenges due to disparate databases. Similarly, processes needed to be coordinated across multiple departments to remove duplication of effort. Most of all, Cathy recognized that traditional budgeting practices prevalent in Corporate America were complex and time consuming. She saw that a more flexible system would help Fortis Health create new budgets and forecasts, making it more nimble to changing conditions.

As Fortis Health wanted to begin forecasting more frequently, it would soon require additional resources to support these increased reporting requirements. To overcome these obstacles and move towards the desired future, the Performance Management Department set out to find a new budgeting and re-forecasting solution.

Q: *Cathy, why did Fortis health move to transform its budget process?*

Cathy Jorgensen: Fortis Health is the oldest national health insurer and a leader in the individual medical small group and short-term medical markets. Due to ongoing competitive pressures, we are committed to continually improving our business and recognize the importance of aligning strategy, operational activities and financial results. Our vision is to create a reporting environment that provides timely and insightful feedback, concerning strategic, operational and financial objectives and to provide tools to support business analysis and decision making, with a focus on business processes and how they impact the entire P&L, not just operating expenses. Fortis Health has moved from a traditional budget process with its entitlement environment to more frequent expense forecasting to reflect changes in the marketplace. We wanted to strengthen the alignment of the financial planning with corporate strategy in terms of general expense, forecasting and as reporting requirements were increasing there was a need to simplify and increase the efficiency of the planning, expense forecasting and activity-based costing processes. We were using multiple databases with over 3000 worksheets for expense forecasting alone. There was duplication of data and activities. We were not able to be responsive to management request and our existing process offered little to optimize performance.

Q: *So how did Fortis chose to address the issues that you just laid out?*

Cathy Jorgensen: To change from a traditional budgeting culture we developed five guiding principles:

1. No forecasting activity should be performed or data reported more than once.
2. Forecasting drivers and metrics should be done by the person in the best position to do so.
3. All data should reside in one database.
4. The solution should be web-based for ease of access.
5. The solution should be flexible to support a rapidly changing marketplace.

Q: *So you implemented a new solution, what does it look like?*

Cathy Jorgensen: What we have implemented is a dynamic operational planning and forecasting solution. It brought all of our spreadsheets into a single application, enabling us to reduce the time and effort for expense forecasting and thus freeing resources for analysis.

Q: *How does the new process work?*

Cathy Jorgensen: New business sales are forecasted and this drives other non-financial driver data, including staff models and general expenses. Our line item cost, product line allocations and P&Ls all flow from the forecast.

Q: *What benefits has Fortis Health gained from this?*

Cathy Jorgensen: Rolling forecasts that span operational staffing and expense planning within the first few days of the month will help us manage our business. The solution has enabled more collaborative financial planning as a single database has eliminated driver data silos. We are creating closer alignments of departments as they have better visibility of the impact of their expense forecast and collaborate for resource allocation. Having a dynamic planning and forecasting solution has facilitated our move away from an entitlement culture in favour of a rolling, driver-driven environment. Financial information now represents operational and strategic behaviours, focusing on processes, not just operational expenses. We are more closely aligning our processes with strategy to enable us to provide multidimensional decision support. Having a web-based application has made it easy for users in all out locations to access and enter information. We are now able to respond quickly in terms of expense forecasting to changes in the business climate and we are increasing the accuracy and the reliability of our expense forecast.

The implementation of the new solution Fortis Health moved to monthly re-forecasting doing away with the annual budgeting process in favour of a more "rolling" environment. The solution also ended the duplication of activities across departments at Fortis Health. Tasks are now accomplished by the appropriate person at the cost centre level, with data "rolled up" through the various departments. Using the web, cost centre managers are able to enter metric data and interact with the system to perform detailed multidimensional analysis for decision support. Closer alignment between departments has also resulted as cost centre managers have better visibility into the impact they have on each other and can better collaborate on budgets and the allocation of resources. This integrated exchange of information gives management the operational information they need to drive down costs in functional areas and further reduce the cycle times in the financial reporting process.

Summing up on what was achieved and what continues to be used in the company, which now trades under the Assurant brand, Cathy Jorgensen said:

> Flexibility to re-forecast and quickly revise plans is important in today's business climate, and especially in the complex health insurance industry. The package we chose met all our criteria for an advanced planning and budgeting application. We look at this as implementing a solution, not simply installing software.

> By replacing our annual budgeting practices with a more rolling and flexible environment, we are able to respond more quickly to changes in the market as well as changes in operational strategy. It greatly reduces the time and effort of re-forecasting. We estimate it will save 2,500 man-hours related to financial planning over the next year.

WHSmith Retail

WHSmith PLC, one of the UK's leading retail groups, is made up of two core businesses: WHSmith Retail and WHSmith News. WHSmith PLC is listed on the London Stock Exchange (SMWH) and is part of the FTSE mid-250 Index.

WHSmith Retail has 542 high-street stores, 200 travel stores at 125 airport and station locations across the UK, and WHSmith Direct serving customers on the Internet 24 hours a day. The high-street business sells a wide range of newspapers, magazines, stationery, books and entertainment products. WHSmith Travel sells a tailored range of newspapers, magazines, books and confectionery products for people on the move. Delivering to 22 000 customers daily, WHSmith News is the UK's market leader in newspaper and magazine distribution. Through its 52 distribution centres across England and Wales, it serves both independent and multiple retailers.

In the late 1990s, WHSmith developed a store budgeting system based on a driver model and workload. A small team of industrial engineers spent approximately a year analysing the working patterns and identifying the 250 most important tasks undertaken in stores. These were analysed by time required and by driver. Drivers are those factors that influence when and how often the tasks are undertaken and how long they will take. Time is influenced both by volume and where the activity is undertaken – depending on the local store constraints. Many factors influence the cash flow and resources required for a store. Sales mix is one key area. The volume and value can be very different for different products. WHSmith has 27 different product areas that it forecasts for each store for every month. Activity is driven by volume, whether the product is delivered directly from the supplier or centrally distributed by WHSmith, whether the goods are sold or returned, and the type of return that has to be made. These forecasts and activities have to be integrated to create an accurate budget. However, there was difficulty in that it was hard to maintain. They were using spreadsheets and the data in the supporting computer system got out of date, so over time the system fell out of use.

Since then, WHS has invested in redeveloping an operation-based planning system. In 2003, the organization initiated a project to improve their staff cost control. By September 2003, they had started shadowing their existing systems; and in September 2004 a new planning system was used as the basis for all store budgets. Budgets and re-forecasts are produced from the system. The system produces data used as the basis of the demand forecast. This has to be done down to product area to accurately predict the resource demands on the business. These forecasts are then entered into the model and the budget is built bottom–up, taking into account the demand, mix, constraints and times for each store. Two-hundred-and-fifty million calculations are made on top to create the UK business level budget.

The result is a budget and a monthly plan for staffing requirements by department for each store. For smaller stores, these plans are less important as with only half a dozen staff the store manager can often physically see what is happening in and around his store. For larger stores, some of which employ in excess of 100 people, the plans are extremely useful as they bring together the combined wisdom on staffing levels from across the company to give an accurate plan for that store to work to.

One of the advantages that this gives WHSmith is that they can use the model to assess the manpower consequences of change. For example, a decision to increase the "card space" in a store can now be modelled using the system. Sales forecasts will provide the change in demand for the new product mix, and the predictive planning system takes these forecasts to produce the new staffing requirements for the store. It is only a short step from here to take the sales and net profit before the change and to compare this with the sales forecasts and projected manpower costs to produce an objective assessment of the impact the change will have on trading. Further, the rapid calculation of the staffing requirements gives store managers immediate guidance on how they should now allocate their staff under the new layout.

The introduction of the new planning and budgeting system has not necessarily speeded up the process, but it is giving better budgets and operating plans. The result is much more prescriptive in terms of staff numbers and gives a better result. Its introduction has provided much greater ability to undertake profitability analysis at the product level. Previously, the company had visibility of the gross margin, but now the company can see the net costs, after costing in staff time. This allows the company to make a real assessment about promotions, taking into account not just the revenues generated, but also the additional costs incurred.

Building the store budgets bottom–up incorporates a level of detail not previously available. It also sets the level of performance and fixes the costs. To reduce costs, the system identifies the key drivers, such as reducing returns, cutting down on the number of space changes and reducing the number of promotions. This gives store managers a handle on how to manage their stores. As one executive put it, "We are now very, very clear about the parameters we are working to. We are clear about what we are paying our stores to do."

In the financial results released to the 31st August 2005, one key headline reported to the shareholders was that "During the year High Street Retail has delivered £18 million of the 3-year cost saving programme, £3 million more than the announced £15 million target. The business is also on track to deliver the total £30 million target over 3 years." Kate Swann, the Group Chief executive when commenting on the results stated that "In High Street Retail we have improved by 87% versus last year. Our staff has worked hard to manage costs tightly and implement initiatives to increase product availability and choice and to raise store standards."

BDL Hotels

BDL is a privately owned medium-sized hotel group who own and operate hotels under the brands Holiday Inn, Express and Ramada. The company was founded in 1997 and from there it has gone on to develop and buy hotels. In 2005, the company had 660 employees with a turnover in excess of £50 million a year. In November 2005, BDL sold a segment of its business, and is now using this capital to develop more hotels.

In 2004, BDL embarked on a review of its planning and budgeting process. The company had grown rapidly, doubling its size between 2003 and 2004, giving a number of budgeting issues that needed to be addressed:

- The increase in company size and the number of units being managed increased the complexity of the planning and budgeting process.
- Information was not readily accessible and the company was looking for a faster response and great data accessibility.
- The budgeting process was slow taking six months to complete.
- There were problems concerned with the data integrity of the spreadsheets being used. Calculations had to be checked and there was a concern that the formulae being used were not fully understood.
- Version control was a problem. Budget revisions occasionally got confused and management were not always sure that the changes requested had been actioned.
- The detailed budgeting work was lost in the spreadsheets. Updates were hard to implement and the impact of detail level adjustments were hard to assess.
- The business was over-reliant on individuals who had the detailed knowledge to make the spreadsheets work.

There was a belief that better planning and budgeting would improve cost control, facilitate better decision making and improve profitability. To this end, BDL embarked on a project to upgrade their planning and budgeting system. The project involved developing an understanding of the corporate requirement. Through surveying the senior executive team, a short list of tools and features was identified. These were then matched against the industry's software offerings before choosing a package that was tailored for driver-based budgeting.

The project started on 20th June 2005 with a series of workshops, including the operating managers. Through these workshops, a set of business rules were developed that underpinned the business model. The model was then built and completed by 14th August. After this date, users began entering the data to create the 2006 budget (BDL's financial year running from November to October). This approach halved the time normally taken for the planning and budgeting process.

The new planning and budgeting process allows BDL to separate departmental responsibilities into the hotel specialist areas. Many of the services and supplies used by the hotels are negotiated centrally. These central functions could then populate the model covering the agreed contracts and the hotel operating staff were given the information against which to manage. For example, the executive in charge of housekeeping for the group centrally negotiated costs for towels, room cleaning and public area cleaning. There is a planned replacement policy of soft furnishings such as pillows. These rules were then built into the central model. Requirements could be compared against actuals and variances controlled. In addition, this allowed replacement of standard items to be managed in line with company policy, ensuring customer service standards continue to be met.

Cost control relies on managing key performance indicators such as food and beverage cost percentages. At the very onset of the new budgeting process, it was made very clear that these ratios were set by the group with the local operating management having responsibility for delivering them. What the new system does is starkly contrasts those costs that are the responsibility of local management and those managed elsewhere. Managers now have greater insight into the level of detailed planning that is done by other parts of the business, to ensure adequate cost control and consistency of service delivery.

There were some implementation issues. A complex rule caused a real problem as from time to time it "fell over" and required the entire system to be rebooted. This was frustrating to the users as they were locked out whilst this happened and resource was tied up in rectifying the situation. This was resolved when an error in a period unassigned rule was identified, but it undermined the credibility of the system when it was happening. There were also issues with network capacity. The company was unable to get SDSL in their location and so users accessing the Glasgow computer shared a 256k outgoing pipe. This made speed a huge issue for them. This issue was not identified at the outset and was only resolved by installing a 2MB Bonded ADSL solution to speed up the connectivity.

The implementation of the driver-based planning and budgeting approach at BDL is complete, but in many ways, the utilization of the new data is in its early stages, and further benefits are expected to accrue. So far, the organization now has far greater access to data and reports over the web. Key performance indicator reports are produced that compare actual against budget and last year actual. Reports have been developed so that the data is available in a format allowing each hotel general manager to compare their own performance against other hotels within the group. This data is automatically extracted from the system and no longer needs detailed checking and scrutiny.

The introduction of the new business process has also improved the understanding of the budgeting process itself. It has created an "open" environment as performance data is available to all management. This has fostered a sense of competition between the hotel general managers, creating a drive to greater profitability and cost control. These benefits have been particularly influential outside of the finance department.

Overall, both the logic and the data used within the model are working well. The rules that were defined and then built accurately mapped our business process and so the logic of the model is a success. The project team and the consultants did a great job building the system in such a short timescale.

Index